CW00664492

*For Nancy and Bryan
who had a delinquent father.*

'THE FACT IS THAT EVERYBODY WHO STARTS DOING THIS DEVELOPS
SOME KIND OF PERSONA OR IMAGE TO SURVIVE. OTHERWISE IT IS VERY
DANGEROUS TO GO OUT THERE. THE WHOLE THING IS AN ACT. NOBODY
WOULD REALLY SHOW YOU WHO THEY ARE. NOBODY WOULD DARE AND
IF THEY DO, THEY CHANGE THEIR MIND AFTER A WHILE BECAUSE IT GETS
TO THE POINT WHERE THEY DO NOT KNOW WHAT IS TRUE ANY MORE.
THE DICE IS THROWING THE MAN INSTEAD OF
THE MAN THROWING THE DICE.'

TOM WAITS, 1999

We would like to thank the following copyright-holders for allowing us to reproduce their pictures:

BRIAN ARIS
ALAN BALLARD
ROBERT ELLIS
BILL FRANCIS
LONDON FEATURES INTERNATIONAL
TERRY O'NEILL
BARRY PLUMMER

Pictures also reproduced by kind permission of Aquarius and Rex Features.

CONTENTS

LETTER BOMBS AWAY

This is all Pete Townshend's fault, and that 'Sting' who kept urging, 'Write the book Keith — write the book — if you don't write the bloody book I'll do it for you.' If only. This from two massive talents whom I represented for over a decade — nearly two in Pete's case. I am a journalist/press agent who is old enough to remember Max Clifford not single-handedly masterminding Frank Sinatra or the Beatles' career, and football agent Eric 'Monster' Hall being Marc Bolan's plugger not his mentor except in his dreams.

It was Pete who gave me the original idea for this concept after I wrote a tongue in cheek letter to all the individual members of The Who, when they decided that, after fourteen years as their press agent, I was superfluous to requirements when they disbanded. That original letter was based on the pretext that I was at long last able to tell them the truth about themselves after years of frustration and repression as their lackey.

'Why don't you write letters to all your clients?' suggested Pete. 'Tell them the truth. Let them know what you really think of them having been their press agent. It will do you good, and it may even do them good.'

I felt compromised because my press agency had a few years to run into the nineties, but now I can answer the questions — 'What were they really like, and what was your true opinion of them?' Here they are, with love 'From Me To You'. Jagger, Stewart, Hendrix, Townshend, Morrison, Davies, Bolan and The Beach Boys were just some of the superstars who fawned before me as a musical journalist. However, it transpired that many of these I had interviewed for the press and my BBC radio programme *Scene and Heard* were not so humble when I became their hired gun.

Why I ever switched from being a music journalist for ten years, to press agent for twenty-five baffles me, but I am inclined to the whore's excuse. 'It was fun at first and they paid me good money. It also contributed to keeping the small wife, starving mortgage and two children in a lifestyle we did not expect.

My first ever client account on becoming a press agent was Amen Corner, and the first single I worked on was 'Paradise is Half as Nice' which promptly went straight to number one on the January 29th 1969. Piece of cake, this PR! They included the highly talented and underrated singer-songwriter-guitarist, Andy Fair-weather-Low, who now sits on the right hand of God playing rhythm guitar for Eric Clapton.

As more prospective clients contacted me like Manfred Mann, The Beach Boys, Status Quo and The Moody Blues I formed a partnership with another experienced PR called Chris Williams, before breaking away and establishing K.A. Publicity in the early seventies with Alan Edwards, who today has his own thriving music PR company representing David Bowie, Boyzone, the Spice Girls et al.

Super Egos pay for care and attention, and I was soon rolling with the likes of The Who, The Rolling Stones, Deep Purple, T. Rex, The Beach Boys, Jeff Beck, Van Morrison, ELP, Rod Stewart, The Police plus the man who would be Sting.

Over twenty-five years I regressed from representing The Rolling Stones to Orville the bloody duck in the nineties, when I decided it was time to call a halt. I thought ventriloquist Keith Harris should have gone in that direction and his stuffed duck should have been barbecued.

Pop stars and groups have always had a love-hate relationship with the media, who generally play midwife at their birth. Superego knows that without the paparazzi, the publicists and the press they may never get the break or be elevated to the super-star status they covet, so to begin with they play along. The artistes need us to persuade the public and the media to believe in fairies and fiends alike.

It is often image with attitude plus publicity that inflates these talents to megastar proportions and ensure that when you buy the records you subliminally retain a pre-packed impression of the artiste to suit the song and dance. Image plus attitude launched Elvis, The Beatles, The Sex Pistols, Madonna, Oasis and the Spice Girls. It is always the same formula — alienate the adults so they do not understand the message and win over the kids who empathise with the youthful stance and can decipher the loud coded argot of the times.

When it is still a cuddly puppy, the media usually love 'little ego' until it becomes a successful snarling rock and roll Rottweiler. 'Fang' then finds itself under close scrutiny by the press and often becomes resentful and precious over privacy which was not so important when it needed to put its face about at all costs.

Once Superego is established as a celebrity they can now afford to be difficult and withdraw co-operation unless they have an ulterior motive in selling or promoting something. The three most skilled manipulators of the media I have seen over the decades are Mick Jagger and Paul McCartney, who never open their mouths without something to sell, and Annie Lennox, who never opens her mouth except to sing like an angel.

Once the media suspects it is being used, a war of attrition breaks out so that Superego is persuaded to employ a high powered spin doctor to provide a bridge/wall in order to gain publicity without exposing the soft underbellies of their true identities. Exposure can sometimes prove costly if your star is intent on projecting a macho image at odds with their persuasion — George Michael and Michael Jackson spring to mind.

Most rock stars I have known and represented like Jagger, Sting, Stewart and Hendrix were multifaceted personalities who invented another creature which became their on-stage persona. The danger is that the creature can take over the real person so that they begin to believe their own publicity.

It is no coincidence that the only film for which Mick Jagger received any real critical acclaim was *Performance*, which dealt with a popstar's split personality, and was something he well understood. There must be occasions when Mick is tempted to wonder who the boy–girl in the painting in the attic was and who is the ageing, skinny mogul with all the stocks and shares is in the mirror now. As septagenarian George Melly put it so succinctly at the Voodoo Lounge reception to Jagger, 'You have more lines than me on your face.'

'They're laughter lines,' returned Mick.

'Surely nothing is that funny,' trumped the old jazzer.

As a publicist I could seldom tell Superegos the truth, even when asked, because you are usually presented with a finished product and expected to tell the media and them how wonderful it is. Most rock stars are surrounded by minions who are employed to tell them how wonderful they are — there are few true friends and employees who will risk being fired by telling them unpalatable truths. I recall one amusing exception in note form some years ago left by a disgruntled ex-employee which read, 'The Wages of Sting are Death.'

Superego does not want to hear from his PR that six months in the studio and tens of thousands of pounds have not cut the mustard, or that the new album is pretentious crap and the sleeve a disaster. They still 'shoot the messenger' in the music business. A publicist is required to massage Superego — not puncture it. Having been both poacher (journalist) and gamekeeper (press agent) I knew both the requirements of the media and the artiste. They are seldom the same. Illusion is the name of the pop star's game, and revelation is most often the media's aim.

The second album is often inferior to their first, which the new artiste may have taken years to hone as he or she learnt their trade, as opposed to the few months it took to record the follow-up so that the record company can capitalise on the initial success. I would probably not play the new tracks to a deaf, dumb and blind wombat, but you are now buying the publicity not just the music — never mind the quality, feel the face.

Pop music is fantasyland and a star is seldom what they seem or what you read about or imagine. Those journos who write up the stars whilst waiting to socialise with them later in the 'green room' are seldom honest in their opinion because it is not in their own best interests to be so. They will need their famous contact to make money in the future.

You soon learn as a press agent that Superego can have the superficial charm of a dolphin coupled with the survival instinct of a hammerhead shark — 'Cuddly' Cliff Richard and 'Matey' Rod Stewart are in that category — check with an ex-employee or a musician who has worked for them just how nice they are. These long-timers are exceptionally demanding, driven artistes. You cannot expect a massive talent to be universally loved by employees. I came across a Scottish stage hand who worked on the Tommy Steele *Singing in the Rain* touring production. He told me some of the crew loathed him so much they would pee in his rain machine in his absence before he splashed gaily about in it performing the title song.

The stage hand would occasionally delight in mentioning in a loud voice that it looked as though they might have 'A wee drop of rain this evening' in front of the man they considered a slave driver.

Many of my clients I genuinely liked, but the litmus test is, as one of the Moody Blues once put it, 'Would you invite Keith Moon or Ozzy Osborne back home?'

We all wonder at times what keeps some of these stars going, having acquired all the money and fame most of us would realise in a lifetime, and the answer was supplied for me from an unlikely source at a recent BASCA awards ceremony by an old, but immensely popular and charitable artiste who has now sadly passed away. Frankie Vaughan was a man who had his fair share of teenage adulation in the fifties, and gold records galore. At his peak he was starring in movies with Marilyn Monroe, and after he had received an award for a lifetime achievement in showbusiness, he made this emotional but profound comment on why pop stars refuse to give up and grow old gracefully. 'For those of you out there who wonder what is it that keeps us going on through all the good times, bad times and the pain — it is very simple — it is desperation. We will do anything to be loved. *Anything*.'

There may be a suspicion of the spin-doctor's revenge here, but I have written it more in the spirit of an amused 'unloading' of some of the exasperation which is integral to the job of being a press agent. I offer an amused peek behind the mask of the Lone Pop Rangers for the prurient and curious like me. These are merely my opinions and recollections of the good, the bad and the ugly I represented, and perhaps an overdue written reminder to one or two 'pop gods' that they, too, are human.

THE PR MAN ONLY KNOCKS ONCE.

MICK
JAGGER

Keith Altham chats to
Mick Jagger.

MICK JAGGER

YOU'RE SO VAIN, YOU PROBABLY
THINK THIS LETTER ...

Dear Mick,

Always a pleasure to hear from a journalist and an ex-Rolling Stones press agent with an axe to grind eh? Not often we bump into one another these days unless it was when I used to catch you mincing round the Richmond Garden Centre with Jerry (remember her?). I never really thought it politic to confront you and enquire as to how your hibiscus or your clematis was coming along. Leave all that to Alan Titchmarsh shall we?

Remember when we first slept together — remember Nice 1964 — in fact, do you remember anything without the aid of Bill Wyman's diaries? Very mean of him not to let you plagiarise them for the purpose of your own biography I thought — after all what are friends for, other than to be used? Giving back the million dollar advance must have hurt. Not as much as the recent ten million pound divorce from Jerry, of course, or the five million quid demanded for your most recent little mistake.

Meanwhile, back in the bedroom, I know I was not

exactly David Bowie, and it *was* separate beds we were sharing in Nice, but we *did* sleep together when I found myself covering the Stones' European tour for *NME* in the sixties. Twin beds, for those that care. However, I am sure you recall waking me up each morning to the accursed *Beach Boys Greatest Hits* with the pronouncement 'I am an expert on wake up music'. I still suffer from surf sickness to this day — so 'Help Me Rhonda'.

That was the Stones tour during which you pulled Brigitte Bardot in Paris with your schoolboy French — at least, I *think* that's what you used. Bardot was absolutely stunning in 1966 and you also had the lovely 'marbled' Marianne Faithful sitting at home in London warming up the baked beans on toast in Cheyne Walk (she once informed me that was your favourite of her culinary specialities — come to think of it I believe it was her only one).

Your long-term lovers, especially Marianne (who used to get £25 a week housekeeping from you), have always been endearing and since leaving you even 'Her 'Biancaness' has done sterling charity work for the oppressed, tortured and disenfranchised around the world. There, I suspect, went your social, political and spiritual conscience. I even liked your first love Chrissie Shrimpton (even if she did try and sell your love letters to the *News of the World* later) — and I never believed the story about her 'yappy' little dog you allegedly put in the oven late one night because it was keeping you awake.

Jerry Hall always seemed to me to be a glamourous, independent Texan belle with the patience of a saint — albeit not inexhaustable. Now you have scored an own goal in an 'away leg' in Brazil and Jerry's asked to be put on the transfer list. 'Whoopsadaisy then Mick,' as

Keith Richards put it so succinctly on hearing of your new baby. Twenty-two years, of which nine were married, and four children later the unsavoury 'Phantom Marriage' rumours were 'leaked' to the press and you secured a ten million settlement. You are lucky Jerry is a lady.

Having lunch with Marianne shortly before her revealing autobiography was published I ventured it might be difficult to live with some of the unpleasant revelations about your relationship. She looked at me wide-eyed and in that wonderful throaty Marlene Deitrich voice she now possesses stated, 'I don't have to tell the truth do I dahrling?' Quite.

My friendship with your late keyboard player Ian Stewart, who, like me, came from Epsom and founded the Rolling Stones with Brian Jones in the sixties gave me an inside straight into early Stone power play. Remember them — you joined their group in 1962? 'Stu' got the old 'heave-ho' and was sacked because his face didn't 'fit'. Your early manager, Andrew Loog Oldham, used the cynical excuse 'the great British public could not count up to six for a group.'

Shortly before his untimely death in the late eighties 'Stu' and I started on a book which was to be his honest assessment of what happened within the band he started with Brian. His initial opinion of you was typically frank on the ten hours of tape I have with him — perhaps the last truthful voice you heard.

'My first impression of Mick was that he was a supercilious arrogant young sod who was more interested in attention and money than music,' Stu told me. Not much change there then. 'Brian Jones and I wanted Paul Jones who eventually joined Manfred Mann as the Stones' vocalist because he had a better voice and was deeply involved in blues music.

'There was and is, though, something very special about Mick. He has a sort of deadly sexual attraction and he knows just what he wants and how to get it. He is the equivalent of a sexy black hole in space — everyone gets sucked in and nothing gets out. When our original concept of a young white blues band went out the window and it became 'The Keith Richards and Mick Jagger Rock and Roll Band' I was not unduly surprised. Mick usually got what he wanted.'

Stu as he was better known to you all was demoted to 'glorified roadie' prior to your first hit and the decision to sack him blamed on manager Andrew Oldham, but we all know where the real power centre of the band was, don't we? Hands up all those who voted to keep Stu in the band at that time? Loved him like a brother though, eh? Being *your* kid brother has got to be difficult. Being your *kid* must be embarrassing at times. Being your *wife* has to be impossible! Being a *friend* is dangerous.

'Stu' recognised the early signs he might be on the way out when he found his piano mysteriously moved from one side of the stage to the other with out warning: '*Andrew says* we need more room and it looks better there.' Founder Brian Jones was to be the next victim and would arrive to find his mike was not on: '*Andrew says* he does not like your voice.' Jones' multi-instrumental ability was soon surplus to requirements: '*Andrew says* we should keep to the group sound.'

Brian Jones was not altogether trustworthy (the Stones were displeased when you discovered he was surreptitiously extracting an extra 'fiver' as 'group leader' from your early agent), but did he really deserve the humiliation handed out so systematically before he drowned? 'Treating my friends badly,' was something you once admitted as your 'worst fault'. Amen.

Ironically the next casualty was Andrew himself, who became the victim of his own machiavellian work and burnt out before appearing to get you involved with your American power accountant Allen Klein, who promptly outflanked you financially. Another fine piece of selection. Hoist with your own 'bean counter' and worse you helped foist him on The Who and The Beatles who are still trying to figure out the early financial arrangements.

'Stu' used to say that the public's fascination with your diverse sexual image was the result of your perpetual search for your own true identity. Once you had found yourself, he felt it would probably mark the end of the Rolling Stones. I loved the story he told me of your early androgynous days when you camped around the Edith Grove flat for a few months in drag and eye make-up prior to the release of 'I Wanna Be Your Man'. Your 'Danny la Rue period' he called it.

Clues to your confused sexual appeal and your private life are contained in your own lyrics, but even that is deliberately muddied water. What did you once tell me? 'If you want to find out about me then study my lyrics – but you will not get the complete picture because only I have the key to the code.'

'The Jaggerwock', as I used to refer to your on-stage creation would often get out of control as you threw yourself into the role of being a big, bad, rude Rolling Stone on tour, so much so that doors slammed in faces of friends and foes alike, who were also verbally fried backstage. Bill was always a good target, and Charlie, out of earshot, until you discovered he had a good upper-cut when you summoned him once as 'my drummer'. The normally unflappable and ever patient Mr Watts is the barometer by which the Stones assess the degree of seriousness to a problem. If Charlie's upset, it's a *real* problem.

Even with your head in a bucket, one hand on your hip, lisping with a phoney Irish accent you could never make me believe you were anything other than Mick Jagger hamming it up as Ned Kelly in your first movie. In fact, on your arrival in Sydney wearing an Isadora Duncan scarf and fetching straw hat, the Australian press rather unkindly suggested that the English had entered into a conspiracy and sent Dame Edna Everage over instead. Your major problem is that your acting seems too theatrical, perhaps as a result of having to be so expansive in huge stadia and playing to the gallery.

One of your classic mistakes during my tenure was an aborted role in the film *Fitzcaraldo* in which your rendition of Richard III's famous monologue, 'Now is the winter of our discontent ...' was a stupendous cross between Kenneth Williams and Peter Sellers with a little Julian Clary thrown in – *far* funnier than Richard Dreyfuss in *The Goodbye Girl*.

You made the right decision on *Fitzcaraldo* when you bailed out, after the batteries ran down for your hairdryer and walkman, bitten to death by mosquitoes having being stuck in the jungle location for a month. It brought tears to the eyes when they showed your camp Richard III performance in a documentary about the movie on TV recently.

One of my saddest moments as a journalist during the sixties came when I found myself at the Olympic Studios in Barnes, the night of Brian Jones' death from drowning in his swimming pool. The news was brought into the studios in the early hours of the morning by 'minder' Tom Keylock, and soon reverberated around the control room in whispers. Keith Richards was visibly moved, Marianne was in tears and Charlie Watts retired even further into himself.

It would be unfair to say that you were not upset, but it was a curious mixture of sadness and anger that came over you — and it was anger that appeared to win. When I asked you what would happen now in a general sense, you seemed to relate it to the current recording session and the planned concert in Hyde Park. 'It goes on ... it goes on,' you muttered through clenched teeth.

Keith collared me before I left Olympic Studios and requested that I did nothing to alert the national press that night, or relate your reactions before they had further time to consider and, more importantly, until all Brian's family had been informed. I passed up the scoop. You don't break a promise to Keith and the money was not important anyway. Brian was a 'flake', but I liked him.

In the sixties, before your sense of humour about yourself went on the blink, you also had a talent for fun and mimicry, a prime example of which followed a pithy feature I wrote after a difficult interview with you and Keith for *NME*. Do you recall when Dave Dee, Dozy, Beaky, Mick and Titch were peddling a puerile publicity story about their second-hand van which they had bought only to discover it had been in a death crash and was now apparently haunted by the drivers ghost?

'Dave Dee on the phone for you from Heathrow Airport' announced our *NME* receptionist. 'Ullo, Keef, its Dave — we seen it again — you'd better get your notebook,' said the voice. There then followed a boring diatribe from 'Dave' about the ghost's materialisation and how it had floated in one side of the van and out the other while attempting to seize the wheel and kill Dozy in the process.

After fifteen minutes of note taking I smelt a rat, and my suspicions were confirmed when you dropped the fake voice. 'It's Mick, we're at Heathrow on the way to America,' you sniffed. 'Keith and I just read your interview with us — very funny — don't do it again.' Click.

Remember the fog on the main road to Aylesbury Granada in the early sixties, when Stu used to drive the old battered Rolling Stones Bedford van when you were co-billed with The Ronnettes and we spotted Brian Jones in his Ford Galaxy emerging from the 'pea souper' heading the wrong way back to London on the other side of the dual carriageway?

Stu hit a kerb in the poor visibility and bounced Keith plus his sleeping bag off the ceiling of the van in the back who collapsed with a theatrical groan. We all thought he was faking until on arriving at the theatre we opened up the doors at the rear of the transit and Keith rolled out unconscious with a lump the size of a pigeon's egg over his right eye.

'Right,' said Stu, looking down phlegmatically at his concussed guitarist and then at you, 'I'll pick up the star and you go and explain to the promoter we are now a trio.' Keith eventually came round but we never found Brian and you played amazingly effectively as a quartet.

Without your ruthless drive and determination, the Rolling Stones would have broken up years ago, or left to Keith they would probably have been the most infamous unfamous band in the history of rock. It was your naked ambition, arrogance, avarice, energy and initiative in assuming control which kept the Stones rolling through the eighties and the nineties.

Those of us who loved the Rolling Stones music can be grateful to you for that, but I know you love control so I never believed it when you told me, 'I never wanted to be manager — but someone had to take decisions.' You were the same man in the eighties who offered me the Rolling Stones label manager's job at a Who concert at London's Finsbury Park Astoria with the caveat: 'I make the decisions.' I declined that poisoned chalice. That was the night you tried to convince me to 'come over' because, 'The Who have nothing more to say — they're finished.' I replied that I owed them the same loyalty I gave you.

My initial meeting with you on being offered the Rolling Stones press representation at the Savoy hotel in the late seventies was also an indication to me of the shape of things to come. Someone had given me the tip that owing to the ill health of your press agent, the late Les Perrin, you were looking for a new PR. At our Savoy hotel meeting I demurred that sacking Les in his present state was hardly fair or politically sound judgement. 'We don't need two press agents,' was your generous response to his years of service. I made a mental note that later it could be me — and it was.

Perrin was a respected and hard-working publicist for the Stones for many years. I pointed out that sacking him might be seen by many as a betrayal and that was bad press and poor public relations. I suggested that if you were adamant about a change you should continue to pay his retainer and take me on board as a foot soldier for now for the Stones tour. You saw the self-interest in this and agreed. Stones employees are notoriously poorly rewarded — it is supposed to be sufficent to breathe the same air as your exquisiteness.

My first revelation on taking the job as the Rolling Stones' press agent was that what I had actually become was *your* press agent, and all matters concerning the Stones went through you. 'Congratulations, I hear you've got the job as Mick's butler,' said my friend Stu when we met in our village pub in Ewell that weekend. The truth of that soon became apparent, because trying to do anything for the other band members seemed to be soaked up in the Stones' office by your PA.

Occasionally I would press you on some matter relating to one of the others. Keith? 'Nah he's not well, off the hook, won't want to be bothered.' (Good excuse for avoiding the only Stone with enough clout to veto your own decisions.) Charlie? 'Nah doesn't do interviews.' (Half true.) Bill? 'Let him get his own PR — he's boring anyway.' (Untrue.) 'Ronnie does what we tell him.' (True, at least then.)

You made it clear to me from the start as your PR that you were not interested in talking about semi-intellectual nonsense concerning your songs to the press, and that those who came into 'the presence' armed with cuttings and quotes on things you were alleged to have said or done ten years ago could expect short shrift. 'The deal' was an understanding that they helped to promote the new album or the new tour and you gave them a few stories and opinions to spice up the interview. 'Got me long hair and me couldn't-care-less attitude and me sarcastic responses — so let's go,' you would sniff.

Those journalists who expected you to lay out your private life for their edification were likely to be hugely disappointed, and neither did you take to being patronised. One young reporter who suggested you might just be 'in it now for the money' received a scathing broadside.

'Listen,' you admonished, 'you think you are in a position to lecture me about freedom of speech when I know your proprietor personally and he just wants salacious stories or lies that sell more copies of his paper. You have probably already been told the angle he wants. (Now was that a nice thing to say about the late Robert Maxwell?) Let me tell you I have more freedom to say and do what I like than you will ever have. You think I do this for the money — what about the power, the adulation and the fame? I'm a rock and roll singer and I do it because I like it and if I chose to terminate this interview I will and it won't do me any harm.'

In the eighties I organised a tea party for the England cricket team playing the West Indies which included at that time Botham, Gower and Gooch at Eddy Grant's recording studio in Barbados. Later we were watching a spirited game of tennis at the rear of the studio in which you were engaged with a keyboard player who insisted on 'camping up' your somewhat eccentric style by putting a hand on his hip and shouting 'Shut that Door' in Larry Grayson mode every time you missed. He did not last long with the band.

I can still recall the bewilderment on the face of one of our famous England test batsman watching who said to me, 'How the hell he hits a ball I will never know — he is the most uncoordinated human being I have ever seen.' You won quite convincingly. Which was more than England managed.

Perhaps your most 'outstanding' cricket memory came courtesy of Keith Moon who was my client at the time. I was with him in Tramps one evening when word came down from upstairs that you were about to make your entrance with Bianca after a day swanning around at Lords. Bianca made the mistake of entering ahead of you down the stairs and a scream like a banshee hit the air as she found herself confronted by 'The Creature from the Black Lagoon' with his trousers round his ankles and an unfortunate paucity of underpants. You dashed down the stairs to the rescue yelling, 'Put it away you mad sod!' An apparently chastened Mr Moon hoiked up his strides explaining, 'I heard you had both been to the cricket and just thought she might like to see my bat and ball.'

Your treatment of press can be abrupt as was the case with the *Evening Standard*'s James Johnson in New York in the late seventies following an interview I arranged subsequent to Keith's latest bust for which there was a potential jail sentence hanging over him in Toronto. 'I see you are playing guitar on stage now for the first time,' James opened languidly. 'Does this mean you're practising for when Keith goes down?'

'That's a very rude question, James,' you leered, arose from your seat on the floor, disappeared into the bathroom and never returned. Keith remained and let it go over his head. He seemed to think it was a quite a good question.

The 'Emotional Rescue' press launch in 1980 on which I was engaged, was another 'tour de farce' for which EMI Records had splashed out over £50,000 for a reception, including the erection of a 'MASH'-like hospital unit and tents in the grounds of the Chelsea Barracks in London, with hot and cold running nurses, booze, food, plus army first aid kits. Unfortunately you were the only one who turned up in the morning at the Stones office for the reception.

Keith Richards and Ronnie Wood had apparently gone 'walkabout' in America, although we were filled with false optimism at one moment when Keith's luggage arrived at Heathrow and appeared to be circling the roundabout in free-fall but with no sign of 'The Riffmeister'. Bill was fogged in in France but trying to get a flight out, and good old reliable Charlie was manfully stuck somewhere on a motorway and unlikely to make it in time. 'What shall we do?' you moaned.

My feeling was that without a quorum we did not

have a band, and without the band it was not a Rolling Stones press reception. I cancelled it with three hours to spare and EMI swallowed the bill. Punctuality was never a feature with the Stones, and there was always this silly unspoken 'pecking order' game with you and Keith vying to turn up last at any function. The maxim seems to be: stars are always late; musicians like Bill and Charlie always on time.

One of the funniest although frustrating moments of my term of office as your press agent came about when John Blake, then a columnist with the London *Evening Standard*, rang to forewarn me that he had been 'press-ganged' to 'doorstop' Keith Richards, whose ex-girlfriend Anita Pallenberg had been implicated in the bizarre sexual-Russian roulette death of a boyfriend in her New York flat, and that he had been told to fly to Paris and confront Keith.

I immediately rang your PA in the Stones office to warn her to get a message to you and Keith that Blake was on his way and why. Then I rang Paris where you were recording and left more messages with assistants and a request to ring me. No response, as usual. Two nights later Blake enterprisingly bluffed his way passed your security and into the Stones recording studio in Paris where he self-consciously propped up a mixer whilst surveying Keith through the control room window on a stool playing guitar. You regarded him with the befuddled air of one who knew he had seen that face somewhere before but could not quite place it. Finally you sidled over to enquire of the interloper: 'Got the stuff then?'

Once Blake had embarrassedly explained that he was not 'the delivery boy' you were expecting and who he was, you went out into the studio to relay his request to Keith who could be seen, through the control room window, to take off his guitar, throw away his cigarette, walk into the middle of the studio, lie down on his back with his arms and legs rigidly pointing up at the ceiling. Surveying the 'dead dog' impression for a few seconds you then returned to inform Blake, 'As you can see, John — Keith wants to talk to you real bad.' Somewhat belatedly security then gave Blake the bum's rush. Sometimes I felt smoke signals would get a message to you more competently. Alan 'Mr Tannoy' Dunn, your PA, was always useful though, because I knew if I wanted to get you a message I only had to tell the devoted Alan in confidence.

Do you remember your humour failure over the 'sex change' saga. On a slow news day I would be certain to fend off the usual unfounded rumours of the Rolling Stones retiring or you leaving to go solo. One such journalist from the William Hickey column on the *Daily Express* caught me in a frivolous mood when I confirmed his ridiculous story that you were having a sex change operation in California and that 'it was causing a rift with the rest of the Stones who did not want to tour with a girl vocalist.' Frivolously, I added you were ignoring criticism and picking out some nice new frocks for the tour.

Your 'sex change' was printed as the lead in the William Hickey column the next day, with the postscript that 'I think Mr Altham was pulling my leg.' At best it might be deemed unfortunate that the postscript was omitted in the American news reports and you rang me outraged from Los Angeles. 'It was a joke,' I explained.

'Well its no bloody joke here,' you fumed, 'I've got the entire American Media ringing me up about it.' Click. Somehow it made it funnier.

Your recent excuse in the press about not doing the British '98 tour as it would not be 'fair to the road crew' who would have to pay Gordon Brown's retrospective new tax had me and Bill Wyman in stitches over lunch recently. Masterful piece of 'spin' by your current PR Bernard Docherty. I would have loved to be a fly on the wall at your next *tête à tête* with Cherie and Tony Blair. New Labour meets Old Meanie.

Just in time, and of course and in no way influenced by ticket sales and the bad publicity of your impending divorce, you suddenly remembered you had accrued approximately £250,000 in interest on tickets sold for the 1999 Wembley concert during the year's postponement and made a rare gesture to donate it to charity on behalf of the group. What charity? By the way, why was there a six pound surcharge on all so-called VIP tickets not shown on the ticket, and where did that go? Just curious.

There was one story which puzzled me in a recent biography by Christopher Andersen, attributed to me which I found perplexing. The story which was to illustrate your 'carefulness' with money said that I took a cab with you in New York and you tipped the driver a quarter. Now, I have never taken a cab with you in New York. You were always driven or in limousines and I have never seen you pay cash for anything. You seem to wander through life like the Royals — cashless. A 'quarter' indeed, the very *idea* of such extravagance on your part! That sort of thing could give you a bad reputation ...

JAGGER SACKS HIS PAL ran the *News of the World* story after my four-year tenure was terminated. Well, of course, I never was your 'pal', although I had known you for twenty years. And apart from the wife, the band and the hangers-on I'm not sure I ever actually met a 'pal'. I sat disconsolately in the Green Man pub in Ewell that night of my dismissal with Stu after getting the bad news from your label manager.

'Why would he do this at a time when everything is going so well? Why would he do this when I have three front-page colour supplements set? Why would he do this without a personal word to me after all these years? Why would he not even give a reason for it?' Then I caught a look in the eye of my friend who had founded the Rolling Stones with Brian Jones and been sacked just prior to their breakthrough. How? Easy.

As one half of an extremely talented song-writing team, and a singer with a distinctive voice who poses better than he dances, you might just consider giving more credit to the Stones who have always proved themselves bigger than any individual in it, as your solo efforts have proved. Then again you might not. Could it be that you believe *you* are the Rolling Stones?

You remain the greatest on-stage rock performer of all time, confirmed to me at your Shepherds Bush Empire concert this year, and the Stones still cut it — pity about the dodgy brass section but at least Keith seems to have learnt to sing now — so look out. Not sure about the healthy, beefy black bass player though — he hardly fitted in with the ageing, emaciated, white twig insects on a small stage, although I did notice you have grown a bicep — congrats. Bring back Bill I say — but you will need chains.

I had fun interviewing you, watching, listening and being behind the scenes with the Rolling Stones over thirty years. Like the first time you played the Albert Hall in the early Sixties for which the Stones opened and the Beatles closed the 'Pop Prom' (Brian dead-drunk, face-down appropriately in the coleslaw in the Sir Henry Cole Room). Being on stage at the free concert at the end of the sixties in Hyde Park for Brian Jones was another memorable moment. And the three days with the Rolling Stones Rock and Roll Circus with Lennon, Clapton, Tull, Taj and The Who were magic. There was also the unforgettable gig you did at the Marquee club at 100 Oxford Street with Beck, Clapton and Townshend as a tribute to Stu to mark his death in the eighties. I loved the pseudonyms you used to do your secret club gigs, like 'The Amazing Winos' and my favourite 'The Biff Hitler Band'. Best of all was the evening when, unbeknown to you, I sat outside Eddy Grant's studio, a beer in my hand under a warm, balmy, starry Barbadian sky, an audience of one listening the Stones work the new numbers for your *Steel Wheels* album.

For many years, after a few beers at a party and like millions of other fans, I would skip about doing my sad Mick Jagger to 'Satisfaction' on the stereo. Don't do it any more — bit embarrassing at our age don't you think? No? Oh well, perhaps if I were being paid your fee I might not either. I prefer to remember you as a vulnerable twenty-year-old with hair like a mop on a body like a bean pole who exuded charm, had a grin like a split coconut and thought blues music was all important.

I still relish the story a journalist relayed to me after I wrote a fiftieth birthday feature on you in the *Daily Express* where my major reservation about you was your preoccupation with the pecuniary. After reading it you apparently turned to your PR Bernard Docherty and asked 'How much did he get for this then?' See what I mean?

Your disobedient servant

Keith

PS

During an interview for *Rave* magazine in 1966 you gave me this priceless quote: 'There comes a time in everyone's life when you look around and say what have I done with all those years? If all you have gained during your lifetime is a vast amount of money and absolutely no spiritual insight, no answers to the questions of life and death which really matter to anyone, then you have gained nothing.' So how is the balance sheet?

STING

Two Englishmen in
New York.

STING

THE TALE IN THE STING

Dear Sting,

Of all the superstars I represented, you are the most likeable and curious contradiction. After fourteen years of doing your press from the early days of 'Roxanne' in 1978 with The Police to your solo albums like *Ten Summoner's Tales* in 1993, it is still an endless source of amazement to me that someone with your intelligence, compassion and humour can emerge seeming to be such a humourless prat in the press ... when you really are not.

It was just such a misguided notion which caused the appalling Rod Stewart to carve into the table-top of the Lear Jet which he had hired and discovered you were using next: 'Sting how come you ain't got no sense of humour you cunt?' To your credit you were less offended than staggered with the mentality of a middle-aged multi-millionaire rock star who would spend all that time painstakingly carving such a piece of juvenile graffiti. However, you find challenges hard to ignore.

Following this incident, Mr Stewart's iron security gates outside his Hollywood home were mysteriously assaulted by two shadowy figures in balaclavas (one bearing a passing resemblance to you), who drew up in a rented car and padlocked forty feet of heavy-duty anchor chain around the palings, thus jamming the electronic gates. 'Who ain't got no sense of humour, Jock?'

This mistaken perception of you in the UK press remains predominantly that of a vain star who is so rich that he does not notice eight million pounds being stolen out of his bank account, preoccupied as he is with global conservation and encouraging us to join worthy causes like Amnesty International. If you happen to possess a well-developed sense of social responsibility it is, of course, easy to make someone look pretentious. How does the slogan embroidered on your sofa cushions read again — 'No act of kindness goes unpunished'?

In fact, you are well able to laugh at yourself as this humourous exchange in court over your embezzlement illustrates: 'And tell me, Mr Sumner, is it true that you were once employed in a tax office prior to your musical career, and nevertheless did not notice a discrepancy of this magnitude?' asked the Defence. 'I think that is why they sacked me,' was your response.

Most of the Media have it in for the 'do-gooder', especially when you emerge from the background of punk and rock music. It is an excuse that some stars offer for being uncharitable — 'not good for the image, man.' It is no excuse at all. Your public support of Amnesty International and the Rainforest Foundation (enabling the Indians to own their land to live on) is estimable but somehow you still manage to get yourself branded as a 'tree hugger' or a 'crank'.

I have always felt, despite denial, that it is your strong Newcastle roots and working class background which gave you the strength and determination to succeed. Resolution and combative strength of purpose are typical Geordie traits. The key to your somewhat contrary nature, though, is well illustrated by your love–hate relationship with your background. You worked on your Geordie accent and shook it off like a rat with fleas whilst apparently disowning roots which you seemed to regard as too restricting for your vaulting ambition. You have the rare talent, however, of being able to turn an apparent 'liability' into an asset. You managed, for example, to expiate your feelings over your parents' death with the beautiful *Soul Cages* album and your adoption of a nickname given to you by your Geordie mates who ridiculed the black and orange striped jumper which made you look like a wasp was another sneer you turned into a cheer — and 'Sting' was born.

There was a good story overheard at a charity dinner where your wife was placed next to HRH Princess Margaret who began to tax her on what your real name was. Trudie patiently relayed the story of how you became 'Sting' one more time.

'He has never liked the name Gordon, and this was a fun nickname given to him when he was teenager,' explained Trudie patiently. 'All his family called him "Sting" and even his children and grandmother call him "Sting", and so *I* have always called him "Sting". There was a considered pause, and a smoke ring, as she of the par-boiled 'piggies' gazed into space momentarily and then commented tersely, 'Pitah', before talking other business.

You will allow yourself to fall victim to your own intellectual conceit by assuming all reporters can be won over by erudition and intelligence when most just want a story that will keep them in their jobs. They appeal to your intellect and off you go, seduced into an erudite discussion on anything that can be taken out of context and used to make you appear pretentious later. You tend to wear your integrity on your sleeve.

Once you found an 'artistic' photographer who 'painted with light' and persuaded celebrities to run about like chickens flapping their arms and persuaded you to wear something that looked suspiciously like your mother's old shower cap. It was 'art'. I regret to say the 'chicken' photos looked like a case of 'The King's New Clothes' to me, but no one was prepared to criticise the 'art' except your iconoclastic manager, Miles, who entered the fray as usual like a bull in a china shop whilst unbeknown to him your sensitive photographer was crouched under a table in the same dressing room. Hurling the photographs over his shoulder and about the room Miles bellowed, 'Congratulations! You have finally discovered a photographer who can make Sting look bad.'

Not only were you talented, rich and intelligent but you were insufferably handsome pop god material. Creative, good-looking, rich, intelligent and ambitious. No wonder Stewart Copeland and Andy Summers in The Police were sensitive. Your attitude was, 'They always knew I was in it for me and they did all right out of it anyway.' To be fair you never made it a secret that you were lurking in the shadows of the group. You were nothing if not painfully honest about your ambition.

I found the best photographers like Brian Aris and Terry O'Neil, and you became a rock icon to millions as you made front covers. Subsequently I tried you pull you back into the confines of The Police to maintain a group unity, but you had bolted and you loved it. The Constabulary was dead — long live the Chief Superintendent.

I have always enjoyed my party invitations to your

tiny little bijou residence, for which you seem to have acquired Wiltshire as your back garden. Your 'Wooden' Wedding Anniversary party two years ago was a cracker at which I managed to enquire of a guest in the twilight of the garden whom I intoxicatingly thought I recognised from an old rock group, 'Who are you playing with now?' and illicited the amused response, 'Do you know I am not sure,' as he wandered away shaking his head. That proved to be double oscar-winning actor Tom Hanks (I thought he looked familiar), although I did recognise Dustin Hoffmann before bewildering him about how a young Paul Simon (one of his close friends) had asked me to manage him in the early sixties before teaming up with Garfunkel. 'You might mention to Paul that he still owes me two shillings and nine pence for a shepherd's pie with double veg I bought him in the Brewmaster Pub in Leicester Square in 1964,' I added before the tiny talent glazed over, moving on to dance with his pretty daughter.

I also introduced my partner Adelaide to a friend and she distinguished herself by talking about gardening to him for half an hour completely oblivious as to who he was. 'Who was that charming young man,' she finally asked as he departed for the drinks tent.

'Oh, that was Eric Clapton,' I sighed. 'A guitar player of some sort.' All cats are grey in the dark.

Best moment at that party was with our mutual friend Reg Presley (whom I saddled with his surname in the early sixties — lucky you didn't know me then — you might have become Bing Sting or Sting Sinatra or even Elvis Sumner), who had played at your wedding with The Troggs, taken a mystified look at the exotic Indian dance troupe doing the cabaret, and stated in his best perplexed Hampshire drawl, 'Ee loikes awl this sort of thing, don't ee?' Ee do indeed, Reg, but ee do give good party.

Due to the frugal definition of your fifth wedding anniversary party as a 'Wooden Anniversary', I was able to purchase a modest present in the shape of a little hand-carved Indian prayer stool which collapsed flat like a child's deck chair. I wrapped up my flattened wooden gift with a little bow and left it addressed appropriately, I thought, 'To The Woodentops' in the baronial hall with rest of the Gold, Frankincense and Myrrh.

Three days later I received a thank you card, which I have kept to sell at Sothebys at some suitable juncture, which says, 'Dear Keith, thank you for the "toboggan". We cannot wait for it to snow. I am going to call it "Rosebud". Love Sting and "Witchypoo"'. No act of kindness ...

Your wife Trudie has remained 'Witchypoo' to me since I first saw her play 'First Witch' in the production of *Macbeth* which featured your first wife Frances Tomelty in the seventies. What a misguided piece of production that was, with all the witches dressed up to look like Kate Bush, and Peter O'Toole playing the title role in the hopelessly grand manner of Sir Donald Wolfitt, plus Dudley Sutton, who usually played dubious cockney characters, haplessly miscast as the handsome Scottish hero Macduff — looking as though he we were about to declaim, 'It's a fair cop and no mistake, guv'nor' during the duelling scene.

The entire cast of *Macbeth* had apparently poured buckets of red paint over themselves because the 'potty' Princess Margaret had allegedly suggested at a run through that there was not enough blood. Brian Blessed who played Banquo, supposedly invisible as the spectre in the banquet scene, was dripping with so much red paint, that, despite cries of 'We see him not,' caused fellow thespians frantically to wrench their costumes out of his paint-bespattered, ghostly path.

The only performance of note came from Frances as Lady Macbeth (First Witch was, of course, exemplary) but the play was a publicity disaster of such magnitude (The *Evening Standard* devoted its front page to the crucifixion) that people clamoured to see if it was as bad as the critics had said and it played to packed houses every night.

Your wife Trudie is one of the most formidable and entertaining women I have met (not many back your manager down, and just try saying 'no' to her fund raising for charities), and can also be one of the funniest. I shall always cherish her ad lib when you were attempting to hang a painting of yourself over the mantlepiece in Highgate one Christmas with your patient young son Joe pretending to enjoy helping Daddy by holding the hammer below. If you had seen the faces he was pulling with your back turned, up the ladder, you would have died. Wonderful mimic is Joe — he does a great 'Sting'.

Trudie tried vainly to explain your self-portrait did not fit with anything else in the room and suggested you hang it in the bathroom. 'You can take down the print of Salvador Dali [the famous self-portrait he titled 'The Great Masturbator'] and put it there,' said Trudie and added, 'After all, it will just be replacing one wanker with another.'

Your single mindedness and determination is both your great strength and weakness. It does not make you a bad person — just obdurate but then without that competitive streak where would any rock and roll star be? And look where it has got you — a rich, multi-talented multi-millionaire — but are you happy? Of course you are — you lucky swine!

Confrontation is something else that you relish as the other two 'Policemen' discovered when it came to tough decisions. It was not long before they discovered they had a rock and roll cuckoo in their midst who was prepared to throw the others out of the nest. The dispute over the decision to release 'Every Breath You Take' was a classic example of something that Stewart Copeland felt was not in keeping with the group identity. You knew it would do for you and make number one. You were infuriatingly correct.

Stewart Copeland would lay down a drum track for 'Every Breath' in studios at Montserrat only to discover that you had wiped it out later. The fights were sometimes verbal *and* physical, although masked as being simply 'boys behaving badly' — like in New York where you and Stewart tussled on stage at a sound check in front of me, and you wound up with a cracked rib. It was playing for keeps.

Your most bizarre physical confrontation was your fight with your own creation on the film set for *The Bride of Frankenstein* where your relationship with the actor Clancy Brown who played The Creature might best be described as acrimonious. The fight scene in which The Creature breaks loose and proceeds to beat you as Dr Frankenstein over the head with a plank was played with much relish by Clancy who insisted on several re-takes until you finally warned him that one more over-zealous smack on the head would have repercussions. It did and we were treated to the sight of Dr 'Frankensting' and his creation rolling around on the set trying to beat the shit out of each other until the crew separated you both.

It is rare for you to walk away from a challenge, although I can remember one over Stewart's ill-judged recital of a bad review for *Brimstone and Treacle* in the studio which caused you to walk out of a reunion recording session. You felt that as you had been invited to participate in an event which would help the others financially you did not have to put up with being publically humiliated in front of strangers.

The kind of result which makes a nonsense of criticising your single-minded approach was amply illustrated when you once made bold to show me a cheque you had received for 15 minutes work with Mark Knopfler at the Air Studios in Montserrat back in the eighties where you both happened to be recording. Knopfler, who is a fellow Geordie, rang you at your hotel to enquire whether you would put a backing vocal on a song he was recording with Dire Straits. You agreed and did the song in two takes in half an hour.

After the session, Knopfler asked if you would accept a couple of points on the song when and if it were released or whether you would like a gift or a session fee. You shrewdly went for the points. A year later the song proved to be the multi-million selling single 'Money for Nothing', and your first royalty cheque as a backing singer which you showed me was for 'ONE MILLION DOLLARS' — with more to come.

It is ironic that I helped initially to establish you as a rock 'n' roll idol like Mick Jagger or Paul McCartney when you were far from it. You have always secretly abhorred rock 'n' roll music. You are a self-confessed 'jazzer' from your roots with early Newcastle jazz bands like Last Exit, and your real idol is Miles Davis — despite your claim to have grabbed a handful of Paul McCartney's hair in a mob scene outside the Newcastle City Hall as a kid when the Beatles appeared there.

I loved the story that you told me concerning the meeting with your idol, when your sax player, Branford

Marsalis, took you along to one of Davis' later recording sessions in New York where he was cutting a collection of numbers under the title *You're Under Arrest.* You were number one in the US with 'Every Breath You Take', but Davis was unmoved by your fame. When you were introduced to him he fixed you with a steady stare and asked 'You speak French?'

You stammered a perfunctory 'Un peu' and were press-ganged into doing a translation of the 'miranda rights' for his CD in Europe for which you had to keep ringing Trudie back in London for help when you ran short of vocabulary. Proudly presenting your efforts later to Miles you were asked to read them for recording and got a grunted thanks and a prompt bum's rush from the studio once your usefulness had evaporated. Still, somewhere there is a Miles Davis album with you reading the rights in French and that, as they say, is 'cool'.

There was already something contradictory about your image when you arrived in the mid-seventies in my office in Old Compton Street on your push-bike as a not so young punk with The Police — blonde spiky hair, ripped tee shirts plus combat boots. You were charm personified, but I could not help recalling Peter Pan's advice — never smile at a crocodile. Even your classic romantic pop hit 'Every Breath You Take' is not what it appears, and you confessed to me that, 'It is actually a nasty little song,' written when you were feeling particularly fraught over your divorce.

It was apparent to me from our first meeting that you were not just *hungry* for success — you were ravenous. Nothing was going to stop you succeeding and although the predominant impression was charm on two wheels, there was a strong ruthless streak. You were unstoppable. If you had gone public I would have

taken out shares in you there and then. I had seen that
desire and that hunger before, and you were the closest
thing I had seen to an odds-on favourite to succeed for
years.

You and I had already discussed my relinquishing
your press representation in the nineties — indeed I had
already made it plain on a number of occasions that I
wanted out of the publicity circus and whenever you
felt the time was right to let me know. Termination was
served up by Miles with his usual subtlety and tact on
the phone from New York, and my 15-year association
with you severed along these lines. 'Altham how are
you — how is your wife, your kids, your gerbil, your
business? By the way, Sting says you're fired.' An hour
later you were on the phone apologising profusely with
an embarrassed, 'You didn't deserve that — but you
know Miles.' You softened our already-discussed mutal
parting by sending me a first edition of Dicken's *Our
Mutual Friend* as a parting gift from you and Trudie,
which was typically kind and thoughtful.

I found Miles Copeland's combative and aggressive
American style of management impossible in the early
days of my representing The Police. After just a few
weeks I informed you that much as I liked the group, I
could not put up with any more GBH of the ears from
Miles who seemed under the impression that 'Manners'
was an English butler and 'Etiquette' was a French table
napkin as he bellowed his weekly instructions down the
phone like an enraged rhino.

'Godammit, Altham, why isn't Sting more famous
than Elvis Presley yet? Why have you not got us the
front page of *Time* magazine? Why aren't Andy and
Stewart getting as much space as your other clients like
The Who and the Stones? Why are you not working,
quicker, faster, cheaper, longer and why are you still

allowing the sun to set in the west when Sting is in the East. I want the press to be bigger, better, and more praise — *much* more praise — for me ...'

After ten minutes of this I would place the phone in the top right-hand corner desk drawer and Miles would carry on ranting to the drawing pins and paper clips non-stop for fifteen minutes before drawing breath and ringing back, mistakenly to claim that he had been cut off. I would look in the drawer 'No, Miles, you are still there.' It was of course lost on him — Miles does not have a sense of humour when it comes to making money.

Driven to distraction, I eventually gave you an ultimatum that, although I loved the band, I could not cope with Miles and his belligerent style, and would have to resign the account. 'Leave it to me and just talk to the group,' you said to my astonishment. I did, and Miles simply went away for a number of years. I was not ungrateful.

Your instruction, however, was an indication as to where the real power was emanating from within The Police at such an early stage. Miles, it should be said, is in fact a very good business manager, but not great at any form of public relations or little things like conversation, and his political stance makes it difficult to establish any kind of rapport unless you happen to be to the right of Attila the Hun. Occasionally it even proved a problem for you.

There was a moment of sheer farce which spun off a TV show in which Miles demonstrated quite convincingly that most so-called punks like Johnny Rotten were just opportunist little capitalists, but went a step too far when quoted verbatim later to the effect that you were really only a socialist until you got your royalty statement. You were not best pleased and there was the possibility of a real split for which Miles hurried to Ireland, where I and a small press contingent were with you on tour.

Backstage, in a group which contained U2's Bono and his wife, I was astonished to witness Miles launch one of his infamous right-wing political rants upon the head of an ultra-left-wing journalist I had with me. I tried to stop him to no avail, and later, when we sat behind the journalist on the coach, he leant forward and asked him conspiratorially how the new album was going.

'Miles, who do you think you have been talking with?' I asked.

'Paul McGuiness — U2's manager,' responded Miles.

'Wrong,' I said. 'That is Gordon Burn of the *Observer*.'

Miles turned whiter than his hair. 'Do you think you could explain that everything I just said was off the record?'

Initially, I knew I could establish you as a front-page star and the media would swallow the 'super-punk' camouflage at least for the time being. Your other two punk pretenders in the band were a bigger problem. The talented and often underestimated veteran guitarist Andy Summers (pushing forty at the time) I had last witnessed as a hippy with the truly cosmic Zoot Money's Dantalians Chariot, not to mention very unpunk-like stints with the avant garde Kevin Ayers and Soft Machine.

The all-American boy Stewart Copeland, who was previously the drummer for Curved Air, had married their thigh-booted vocalist Sonja Christina and had as much in common with the Sex Pistols as Ronald Reagan. Still I had The Stranglers on my books at the time, and they were no spring chickens either, so we stuck with the old punk image.

I was never sure whether you were aware that it was Keith Richards who turned me on to The Police whilst I was travelling with the Rolling Stones in America as their PR. Every time I passed Keith's room he would drag me in and ask whether I had heard his demo disc of 'Roxanne' which Andy Summers, whom he had known as a 'New Animal' playing with Eric Burdon, had sent him. I would reply that he had played it to me yesterday, and the day before, *and* the day before that. 'Wal come and 'ere it agin,' leered the The Human Riff, who knew talent when he heard it and so by the time I got back to Britain I had been brainwashed into taking on The Police as clients by Keith Richards.

There is no question that you are a talented actor as anyone who saw you in *Plenty*, *Stormy Monday* or *Lock, Stock & Two Smoking Barrels* would have to testify, but then there were misfires like *Dune*, *Bride of Frankenstein* and *Brimstone and Treacle* which were not in your range. You could not resist a challenge. You even successfully played Broadway in *The Beggar's Opera*. And won in extra time.

You are a walking, talking, singing paradox. A rock star who is really a jazz singer. A hero figure who loves playing villains. A dedicated family man who sometimes finds his own Newcastle background too painful to embrace but gratefully accepts an honorary doctorate from the local University. A self-centred rock star who genuinely loves his family and makes it a priority. During the fourteen years I represented you I cannot recall a single incident when you accepted an offer from any paper however exalted, which included making use of your home or children for publicity purposes. As a member of the paparazzi you would be well advised not to try and snatch a picture of the children while Dad is around.

Your act of kindness and charitable behaviour are sometimes misinterpreted but always sincere. A few more like you would do no harm in this business. There are your philanthropic acts (like your donations to innumerable charities and the local Newcastle music school run by an old mate) plus giving your time to functions like that at Shakespeare's Globe Theatre this year organised by Trudie for the Buddhist meditation garden adjacent to the Imperial War Museum.

Sometimes your charitable and friendly nature can cost you, and I recall one time walking a few blocks with you and your tour manager Billy Francis in New York to one of your concerts when as we approached the front of the hall, we were accosted by a young black lad who gave you a high five and a great line in bullshit. 'Sting my man. How you doing? Good to see you. Welcome to New York. I hope you have a great concert. You a real talent and we always happy to have real talent in New York ...'

You smiled and after a good few minutes gave Billy the nod to slip him a twenty dollar bill. 'Please, noooooo,' he protested indignantly. 'I never take money from someone I have just met. Ah only accept money from my friends. Only from my friends. I just wanted to wish you well.'

You shook his hand and apologised for doubting his veracity. The boy waved goodbye as we disappeared round the huge building to the stage door. Just as we turned the corner ahead of us, from the opposite side of the building appeared a familiar figure running towards us waving, 'Sting, *my friend*, how are you doin' — can you lend me fifty dollars?' He got it.

You might be amused to discover Tina Turner's

reaction to a small piece I helped her ghost when she nominated you as her favourite songwriter in the *Guardian*. I submitted the finished piece on her collected thoughts. I appended one little witticism at the end of the piece, but was requested to omit it on the grounds that 'Miss Turner does not swear'. La Turner made this perceptive observation:

> *Some still seem to assume he is on an ego trip of his own invention. Could it just be jealousy that there are some who do not like the fact that he is good-looking, bright, rich, genuinely talented and cares enough about people and the planet to want it to carry on?*

You are also fondly remembered by your school friend, Jim Berryman, as 'the best loser' he has known. He tells the story of a county athletics meeting in which you were the favourite when he slipped on the final bend in the lane alongside you. He crashed to the ground and you stopped, turned and picked him up, thus forfeiting the race and incurring the undying displeasure of your games master. It is this long, strong streak of decency which redeems you every time and just one of the reasons why you are so well loved and respected by your fellow artistes, and by the likes of me.

Yeao

Keith

PS

Did you ever find out why Bob Dylan handed you a bullet for your Fortieth Birthday? Just curious.

ROD
STEWART

Keith and Rod enjoy a kickaround.

ROD STEWART

THE TARTAN TIGHTWAD

Dear Rod,

One of your more unedifying acts is to materialise in the UK during the soccer season in your favourite guise as a semi-professional Scot (born in Highgate, London, 1945), tightly clenching your sporran and affirming undying support for the Scottish team, before scuttling back to your spiritual home in Hollywood after the first defeat, to count your money and add to your priceless collection of antiques and long-legged blondes you have amassed from wiggling your bum at audiences and enquiring 'Do you think I'm sexy?'

Having declared your great passions as, 'Soccer, drinking and women in that order,' none of them seem to have made you hugely happy — and Ronnie Wood's description of your legendary meanness ('tighter than two coats of paint') is an understatement. I liked your chum Elton's jibe, though, when he sent you a £10 gift voucher for your wedding to Rachel Hunter with the instruction to 'buy something nice for the home'.

When your early manager, Giorgio Gomelsky, turned up backstage in 1984 after your not having seen him for 17 years, you barked, 'Where's my eight pounds seven shilling and sixpence you owe me for the gig I did with The Steampacket at the Marquee in 1967?' Just a joke of course. *Just.*

A former grave-digger whose obsession in your Scottish roots is coupled with your hero-worship of old Scottish footballing fogeys like Denis Law and Kenny Dalglish, you once caused soccer club owner Sir Elton John to declare you were only a 'fair-weather football supporter, interested in hob-nobbing with the star players.' That hit the spot. Furious, you threw him out of your limousine that night in the middle of London with the words, 'That's it — Fuck off you cunt.' Just one of the little spats in the eighties between two stars who liked to call each other 'Phyliss' and 'Sharon'.

Some weeks after having been made your PR, we got out on a football pitch with your son, Sean, near your home in LA. You were both dressed in complete Scottish International kit, of course. I have to report, much to my amazement, you were still bloody good at forty-something. You could deliver a ball thirty yards to feet with consummate ease and had excellent balance and ball control. I have little doubt that had you wanted to become a professional footballer as a youngster you would have probably made it.

You told me that you used to come in for a lot of flak when you played soccer in England where you played for your local side. You were not into much physical contact. 'Mainly goalkeepers were the problem,' you said. 'I would go up for a ball and get a knee in the nuts which left me gasping and they would look down and say things like, "You should stick to singing, sonny," and "Don't worry about him, he's only as good as his next record." Then the cheeky bastards would ask me to open the local fête or something.'

The other problem were your musical neighbours in

Windsor, who seem to think the music was more important than the football. 'People like Donovan would come round and I would hide all my guitars but he would find one and start letting me have it right in the middle of *Match of the Day*.'

The most recent casualty from your 'blondeography' when I inherited your PR was your wife Alana Hamilton, quoted as memorably saying of you, 'He will go through life hurting one person after another until he destroys himself.' Your lover, Kelly Emberg, and your next wife Rachel Hunter would have done well to have harkened to that warning.

The other problems I inherited concerned your playing in South Africa to predominantly white audiences ('I saw no Apartheid — perhaps the black people there do not like my music') plus a 'one night stand' with whom you were spotted in Elton John's Rolls Royce for which the excuse, 'It must have been one of Elton's dogs,' was the charmless explanation.

You were also number one on the Animal Liberation Front's shit list for your apparent love of fur, stemming back to the days of good old Britt 'Let's Shop' Ekland, whom you later described pathetically as 'the girl I should have married'. I bet Kelly, your lover, at the time really enjoyed that one. Ekland once memorably promised, 'If you screw with another woman while you are with me, I'll chop off your balls.' Lucky escape there. Meanwhile, you had graciously described your ex-wife Alana as having 'pushed' you into your marriage while she was pregnant.

I blame my whole difficult experience with you squarely on my friend Jeff Beck, who 'sold me down the river' — literally. We were on a Thames cruise boat to help launch the late Ronnie Lane's tour to raise funds for his multiple sclerosis charity 'Arms', along with a few other charitable souls like Eric Clapton, Charlie Watts, Bill Wyman, Stevie Winwood and Ray Cooper. I bet him £100 pounds he would not finish the tour with you to which he had just agreed.

You later endeared yourself to absolutely no one by poncing into Heathrow Airport and blithely announcing 'I am here to help my old mate Ronnie Lane,' grabbing some charitable publicity. This from a man who has had a sister, Peggy, and a Mother who suffered from MS. You seemed surprised, days later at Ronnie Wood's marriage, that other guests like Charlie Watts, Bill Wyman and Jeff Beck who were contributing to Ronnie's show seem reluctant to talk to you about it.

It was ironically a few days later I got the call from your manager, Arnold Steifel, that he was looking for a PR for your tour. I suspect Jeff mentioned me in dispatches. At least with Beck on board I thought it might be possible to have some fun. I was flown out to Los Angeles and we had a dinner in Hollywood where we met and discussed your various problems, amongst which was an acrimonious divorce from Alana which was in danger of causing you great financial distress. Arnold also made the incongruous comment that he felt you had a future in light comedy and that you were 'extraordinarily funny and we have only scratched the surface of his talent'. You made the comment that when you and Jeff Beck played together again after such a long time 'we looked at each other and the tears rolled.' Now *that* was funny.

You were also distressed by tales, no doubt apocryphal, that, since your separation, Alana had mysteriously dropped a ten thousand-pound bracelet down a toilet and had offered one of the expensive oil paintings in your home to actor Jack Nicholson and his wife as a gift. Publicity-wise you felt it was necessary to put your side about the split and get across that you still loved your family and were now in a 'long-term relationship' (long by *your* terms ...) with the beautiful Kelly Emberg. What I never expected was that you would actually make your kids available for a photo session when we came out to do some new publicity shots.

I arrived in Philadelphia a few weeks later with a party of six journalists to review the tour and put them in a holding pattern, whilst I ventured backstage during the soundcheck to pick up the appropriate backstage passes, and to find Beck. As I flitted past dressing rooms, I noted one with your name which looked as though it were decorated for a Sultan potentate, with wall-to-wall flowers, optics, champagne, food, plus carpets and a vaporiser.

The next door, labelled 'The Band', had fewer optics, no flowers and minimalistic food. The next door for the 'Support Band' had just a bottle of scotch and a few beers.

At the far end of the corridor was a cupboard with the name of 'Jeff Beck', which I opened to reveal a dustbin with six cans of Budweiser floating in it, and Jeff in a foetus position rolled up in one corner. He looked up and grinned thinly. 'You are *all* I need,' he said. 'Where's my cheque book.' He had completed just seven gigs out of fifty. The rest of your band had been running a sweepstake since day one to see how long he would last.

My first sighting of you was as a teenage 'Rod the Mod' who would latch on to anything or anybody to make it. You were queuing a for a hot dog at a blues gig on Eel Pie island behind Long John Baldry, whom you addressed as 'Mother' in the early sixties. Baldry was already a pioneer of the white man's blues, and was useful to you as a younger interloper. You were making the transition from Rambling Jack Elliot to Muddy Waters. Baldry had a bit of temper but was a genuine enthusiast and very likeable — he proved more than helpful in furthering your career. We music journalists at the time assumed, erroneously, and due to your camp appearance and the fact you appeared to be wearing one of Dusty Springfield's old wigs (it was cool to look androgynous in the early sixties) that you were John's latest boyfriend. Imagine the man who later established his sexual prowess as the Errol Flynn of rock and roll being mistaken as gay. You certainly tried hard, though, before establishing your macho image, to convince us that there was room for some serious speculation as to your sexual preference.

In the sixties it was just a case of group-hopping, until you found the right mentors. There followed a spell with the Steam Packet which included Baldry, drummer Micky Waller with whom you worked later, and the gorgeous Julie Driscoll, who sadly became a one hit wonder with 'This Wheel's On Fire', and whom I last remember seeing under Jeff Beck at a party.

Next came a period with Shotgun Express, which included drummer Mick Fleetwood and guitarist Peter Green plus the best unsung female singer of the sixties — Beryl Marsden. You were learning all the time and nowhere did you learn more than with The Jeff Beck Group which included Ronnie Wood and drummer Tony Newman.

It was during your subsequent amalgamation with The Faces, who comprised ex-Small Faces Kenny Jones, Ian McLagan, Ronnie Lane and Ronnie Wood, that you got your 'Jack the Lad' tag, thanks largely to *their* sense of fun. Your career took off like a rocket with 'Maggie May', and some sterling support from the redoubtable

John Peel, who even faked playing mandolin on *Top of the Pops* with you, but became less enamoured as you seemed to fall in love with your own image.

I completed several interviews with you during this period and it was remarkable to see the change from the rather fearful figure who would sometimes sing hiding behind the amps with Jeff Beck to the swaggering, pineapple-haired string bean who strutted his stuff now on stage in mustard-coloured 'kacks' and matching boots, waving the mike stand and cake walking in a style vaguely reminiscent of Al Jolson. The Faces infectious camaraderie, and a hit solo album 'Every Picture Tells a Story' instilled an arrogance born of success. Fame was your drug.

Here is a revealing quote from an interview I did with you at the time:

> 'I'm a terrible show off, really. I've always been very flash. I always have to be one up on everyone else. I'm not going to be humble. Too many artistes are making out they are poor and playing the music for the love of it. I mean I love the music too, but I don't think I would be doing it if I were not getting paid.'

The first to quit you and The Faces was songwriter and bass player the late Ronnie Lane, who had a heart-to-heart with me in The Ship in Wardour Street on his departure. 'Rod has stopped caring about the band,' he told me. 'He is not even keen on sharing the same air he breathes with us — if you can help him write a song its OK, otherwise he wants to play the big I am.'

Your best period, both as a great singer and as a songwriter for me was with the two albums which conveyed what being battered, bruised and bankrupt meant with *An Old Raincoat Won't Ever Let You Down* and *Gasoline Alley*. On those two albums you still had a heart to wring, understood what the blues were, and were a rock singer so you could 'sleep late in the morning and get pissed at will'.

Thereafter, you became the pop star, and the man whose great hero was Jolson, another great vaudevillian in the 'Music Business Hall of Hams', although even he drew the line at stuffing himself in silk and tartan trousers and waggling his bum at the audience.

Tim Ewbank and Stafford Hildred's nineties biography ended on an optimistic note for your future with your wife Rachel Hunter: 'In spite of the age difference and the groom's somewhat colourful track record, this looks like one rock marriage which could surprise the cynics and stay happy.' Now we get the latest news on the latest divorce from the latest blonde, the kids scattered in your wake and Rachel taking revenge by posing nude for *Playboy* — the one thing you asked her never to do. You must have upset her somehow. You are reported now as staying home and playing with your train set, and having a new young blonde girlfriend. Wait a minute. I think this is where I came in and Frank Sinatra went out — who was also rumoured to be playing with a blonde and a train set shortly before his death.

Carry on, Jock,

Keith

NODDY
HOLDER

'Ello,'Ello,'Ello.
Noddy and
Keith party on.

NODDY HOLDER

STILL CRAZEE
AFTER ALL THOSE BEERS

Dear Noddy,

You are the classic case of a rock star unaffected by success and never beaten down by the lack of it, who has barely changed from the early seventies when I first did your PR, and when, out of sheer desperation, I turned Slade into skinheads so we could get you the national newspapers.

Always your own man, and now happily prattling away as a Piccadilly Radio DJ and with a promising career as an actor in TV series like *The Grimleys*, nothing keeps you down. You have the same down-to-earth, ribald sense of humour, good-hearted belly laugh and determination to make the best of things whether you are in fashion or out of it. You are the boyo who put the bawdy grin into glam rock and who turns 'Merry Christmas Everybody' into a seasonal hit every year.

You helped make Slade the glam-rock sensation of the seventies with a voice that could splinter the back row of the stalls with or without a microphone. You have the kind of larger-than-life personality which would be the envy of a chief-barker, and you are still the

51

only man I know who has an answering machine message that can puncture eardrums.

My first meeting with you was memorable for two reasons — my chance meeting with a Hollywood icon and the volume at which you played, making The Who sound like The Amadeus String Quartet. It was the summer of '69. It was lunchtime, hot and I was late as I bounced down the steps from my office in Garrick Street running to that seedy little jazz club called Studio 51 over the road where you were waiting to deafen me. I hit the bottom step from my office, wearing my cool new shades, momentarily blinded by the brilliant sunlight and ricocheted off the back of an enormous man standing with his back to me on the pavement.

Looking up I got a glimpse of a grey toupée of the shredded wheat variety, and noted the stranger was, somewhat unusually for Londoner, carrying a stetson. 'Sorry,' I gasped up at the giant, 'I didn't see you.'

The figure turned slowly and gave a famous lop-sided grin. 'It's OK boy,' he drawled, 'I didn't see you either.' I was thirty years old, five feet eight-and-a-half inches tall, and I had just been 'pigmytised' by John Wayne. My hand strayed to my Colt 45, which I had regrettably ceased packing since my eighth birthday, never presuming I would one day be confronting The Duke. To this day I still connect my first meeting with you with my one and only confrontation with John Wayne.

Waiting for me at Studio 51 with his new discoveries was my friend, the late Chas Chandler, whom I had known since his days as a bass player with The Animals and later as the man who managed Jimi Hendrix. His latest discoveries seem to be an unlikely assembly of oiks, and you bore a passing resemblance to Farmer Giles, boasting great hairy sideboards like privet hedges, and eyeballs like ping pong balls. Your toothy guitarist, Dave Hill, was a powerhouse, and the friendly drummer, Don Powell, appeared to be a Martian — at least I couldn't understand a word he mumbled at the time.

The group brain then appeared to be owned by one Jimmy Lea, who played bass and electric violin and had fiddled on the fringe of the National Youth Orchestra. Surrounded by mayhem and maniacs, he bore the pained expression of a highly-strung young man being driven to the edge of a nervous breakdown by the rest of you — a not entirely inaccurate assessment of his subsequent experience over the years.

Chas rounded you up, confiscated your tea mugs, and cajoled you on to the tiny dark stage in the basement, which was covered with black and white framed photos of old jazzers like Cy Laurie, Wally Whyton, Bix Beiderbeck and Ken Colyer whose haunt this had once been. You played for an audience of one, and the sheer power of the volume sent me scampering to the rear of the hall, holding my ears — the decibel level was hellish, but you were musically tight and highly exuberant.

I staggered out of the club an hour later, half deaf and blinded by the daylight. 'I told you you'd like them,' your massive manager grinned as he slapped me on the back with the kind of blow that pushes your spine through to your chest. I seem to recall suggesting that he come back and meet my new friend The Duke but unfortunately he had lumbered back into his mobile dressing room before I could match them up. John Wayne versus Chas Chandler would have been a good fight.

That was the day I took on your PR, but it wasn't easy, and I made a major blunder. I began to promote you as an antidote to some of the more grandiose rock groups around like Cream, Deep Purple and another of my bands ELP who specialised in pseudo-classical musical indulgence and interminable drum solos from Carl Palmer, who usually wound up after half an hour with a cowbell between his teeth. Slade were different. Slade were fun.

Your first single, produced by Chas in 1969, was titled 'Wild Winds Are Blowing', and it left the great British public completely unmoved. However, we made some snippets in the press on the basis that you were Chas Chandler's latest discoveries — a group managed by Jimi Hendrix's mentor was not to be ignored. Generosity of spirit is something else I associate with you and I can recall your saying to me on Chas' death in the nineties that without his encouragement, which was borne of his own confidence in you, Slade would never have made it. 'When Chas was on your side — he never left it,' was one of your memorable quotes. 'He took us from an unfashionable Wolverhampton band called Ambrose Slade and never lost faith in us. He was the most persuasive man I ever met.'

Your second single was a cover of the Mann and Weill composition 'Shape of Things To Come', which was met by the same studied indifference by the public, and press was becoming hard to come by after nearly six months without a hit. So I decided on a publicity stunt for you

What we needed was something current and newsworthy to keep the band in the public eye and to entice the media to run photographs of you as the new young scene-stealers. What was new, young, brash and causing controversy in the media at the time? Skinheads waz! 'What these boys need is to shave off all their hair, buy boots and braces and declare themselves the first skinhead group,' I pronounced slurringly to Chas after a several beers in a West End pub as we discussed a new strategy.

The following day, though, I rang him back and recanted. 'We can't do this to them,' I said. 'They're nice guys, not nasty foul-mouthed fascist yobs.' 'Too late,' laughed Chas. 'We had their heads shaved this morning, and they're just out buying the boots and braces.'

Initially the ploy worked, and I hyped you into the *Daily Express* and *Disc* magazine as the 'rock and roll bother boys'. I even managed to carve another minor niche in pop history by coining the expression 'Super-yob' for Dave Hill, which much to my amazement stuck for decades. Dave is anything but a yob.

The next stumbling block was when the BBC decided not to play your records, considering skinheads to be synonymous with violence and race hatred. Thankfully, nothing could have been further from the truth, but although we had grabbed some attention, we had also been censored. You were phlegmatic about the whole affair. 'I remember doing our first gig as skinheads with Atomic Rooster and Status Quo,' you said, 'with a bunch of other long-haired bands. When we arrived a buzz went round and you could hear the whispers. "Slade have arrived, Slade have arrived!" When we had long hair, no one cared when we arrived or when went home. Now we had their attention. The skinhead thing was a turning point for us.

'In the long term it was an incredibly important because it gave us an edge and there was a shock factor. It was the time when everyone in rock groups had long hair. They did not know how to label us any more. Were we serious, hard-nosed skinheads — we certainly did not look like bubble- gum poseurs?

'We did not go around mugging anyone or smashing up dressing rooms. We looked threatening — what were we? We were a band who had taken a risk and that made both the media and the public unsure and uncertain about us. It meant we were not being ignored.

'It also meant that whilst the girls were all screaming at the pretty stars like Marc Bolan we got the boys on our side. Cos we sure as hell were not pretty. It also enabled us to take a much more masculine stance in our song-writing.'

By the time the third single, 'Know Who You Are', was released in September 1970 and sunk without a trace, I was demoralised and drained. It was then I made one of my greatest PR mistakes and dumped the band. I felt embarrassed about taking £25 a week from a mate like Chas (a press agent with a conscience — now that's what I call an identity crisis) and unable to get space in the papers.

You understood my principle, but made it clear I was wrong and went straight to another PR. It was, of course, sod's law that three months after my resigning the account you should have your first top twenty smash, a cover version of Little Richard's 'Get Down and Get With It'.

You and Jim Lea promptly formed a composing partnership which in just over four years notched up 16 consecutive top twenty singles and put Slade in the Guinness Book of Records as the only band to go straight in the charts at number one with two consecutive singles 'Tak Me Bak 'Ome' and 'Mama Weer All Crazee Now'.

We were now back on terms as 'friends' and I did interviews with you wearing my other hat as a freelance journalist when you told me the secret of your success. 'Jim and I had written songs together when we were in The Inbetweens, but it took us five years to find a formula,' you told me. 'We knew if we could get our live party feel on vinyl then we would be away. We established that with 'Get Down and Get With It', and then Jim and I wrote 'Coz I Luv You' in my Mums' sitting room, but it was only when we went into the studio and put on the clapping and boot stamping that it really came alive. Slade were the "live" studio band.

'We always thought we would make it some day but it took nearly three years of trying to get a foot in the door before we eventually forced it open with the help of people like you.'

It took over ten years before I regained professional representation for you again, but we did enjoy an Indian Summer when your flagging career received a boost after you stole the Reading Festival with your live performance in the eighties, followed by two single hits, 'My Oh My' and 'Run Runaway' in 1983. At least I could say we had hits together, and we always remained friends to the extent that I was invited to appear on *This is Your Life* in 1996.

It was significant in the nineties that the English comedy team of Vic Reeves and Bob Mortimer chose to satirise you in their 'Slade at Home' TV sketches in which they dressed up in all the old flares, platform shoes and glitter which the band were famous for in the seventies. Bob Mortimer explained to you that you were the only band in the seventies who everyone could remember and recognise individually.

'Vic and Bob proved to be really nice blokes,' you told me. 'I've met them a few times and I found their send up funny and flattering in a strange way. I had spent almost a decade walking down the streets with kids shouting 'Merry Christmas Everybody' at me in July, and since Vic and Bob's reference to our eating habits in the fictitious flat I now get 'Wanna cupasoup and some crisps Nod?' when I go to the supermarket.'

You love telling a good story, and one of the funniest concerned a meeting with Vic and Bob in a Manchester hotel lounge when a man suddenly fell from the ceiling in his underpants and ran off. Subsequently they discovered the 'sky diver' had passed out from his stag do the previous night, been stripped by his mates and left in a cupboard. He had awoken, panic-stricken to get to his wedding, stamped through the bottom of the locked wardrobe and broken through the floor to the ceiling below, falling in a shower of plaster and brick dust into your laps where you were having early morning coffee.

Do you remember the surreal occasion which we spent on the borders of Wales, in a hotel, whilst shooting the video for 'Run Run Away' when we were all turfed out of bed, down fire escapes, in the rain, three times by a malfunctioning fire alarm in the early hours of Burns Night?

Refugees in Reception eventually included a band of Scottish Highland Pipers in kilts, the old 'Cool For Cats' and TV wrestling commentator Kent Walton, a giant caber tosser, two dwarves, 12 firemen with axes and yellow oxygen cylinders on their backs, plus the disgruntled TV presenter of *Mastermind* Magnus Magnusson who happened to be in the same hotel. He went out the front doors, pyjamas flapping over his trousers, suitcases packed, muttering darkly, 'It happened last night as well.' A demented Slade roadie suffering from sleep deprivation then appeared for the third time down the stairs with a shotgun tucked under his dressing gown, growling that he was going to 'shoot any bastard Scotsman' he found. It was shortly after that the police arrived and took him away for threatening behaviour. We should have just shot that fiasco and forgot the video. Life was never dull around Slade.

For those of you wondering why it was that you retired, it is really quite simple. You lost your enthusiasm for the road. You felt disagreements had destroyed the heart and camaraderie in the band. Slade went stale and you had the courage to face the fact and forge another career as a DJ and actor. 'We were never the kind of band like Deep Purple who hated one another but could get on different airplanes and stay in different hotels just to make the money,' you told me. 'When the fun and games began to stop then so did the spirit which drove us on, and with it went the inspiration for a lot of the music. I do miss it sometimes, but it became a chore and then it seemed like my whole life was being run around an obligation and I knew there had to be more. I felt like Slade were just going through the motions and there is no point in that.'

Of all the bands I represented, Slade were one of the best to be with, drunk or sober, unless it was Jim's round in which case we laughed and stayed thirsty. There was something peculiarly English about Slade. They were roast beef, black pud and saucy seaside postcard rock and roll. Your sheer Englishness may have been the reason that you never broke America, but you were hot as hell in the UK during the glam-rock seventies.

Dave and Don are now back on the road as Slade II with another singer, but there will never be anyone quite like you and someone should tempt one of the most powerful and distinctive voices in rock to do a solo album that is full of good cheer, beer and bawdy rock and roll. You are a lovely man with a big heart and a big voice, and I can almost find it in my heart to forgive you for calling your son 'Django' — bless you, Susan and him.

coz I luv you

Keith

ERIC
BURDON

Eric Burdon with the original *Animals*.

ERIC BURDON

HAIRY-CHESTED ROCK 'N' ROLL

Dear Eric,

As the old rock and roll warhorse most famously described by the late Frank Zappa as 'the Charlton Heston of rock and roll', you should get some kind of award for having survived so many dodgy managers, crazed ex-wives (Angie, who was tragically stabbed to death in Australia years after your divorce probably being the barmiest) and unpredictable fellow musicians — like Alan Price who went AWOL from The Animals in the mid-sixties in the direction of Joan Baez with a bottle of vodka, just prior to your US tour.

Amongst your disastrous managers in the US was one who distinguished himself by disappearing to Zurich with all your money in a suitcase, and the late Chas Chandler was vindicated somewhat in asserting: 'Eric's problem is that if someone comes through the door with a long-legged blonde under one arm and a bag of drugs in the other, he immediately asks them to manage him.'

The Animals were a band in which there were never two compatible parts, and whilst Chas attempted to dominate group policy (something that served him well later when he managed Jimi Hendrix and Slade), Alan

Price, who had led his own band The Alan Price Set in Newcastle, boozed and sulked when he lost control. The attention seemed to fall on the 'long-haired leaping gnome' up front, as you once described yourself.

Also sidelined were the likeable and underestimated guitarist Hilton Valentine, and probably the only well-balanced drummer in the Universe — John Steel. You were a bunch of malcontents born to destroy yourselves from within, and you were my favourite band of the sixties, the first real blokes' band. I liked the whole dysfunctional bunch of you. Whilst the girls were busy screaming at the early Beatles and the Stones to such a pitch that they seldom bothered to turn on their microphones — which in the Beatles' case never caused me great concern because they were one of the worst live bands I have ever heard — you could attend a club night with The Animals and get a virtually scream-free set of rhythm and blues from a band who could really play live.

My love affair with you and The Animals did not get off to an auspicious start. My first sight of you was in 1964 when you were brought up to my little greenhouse of an office on the roof of Fleetway House where I was working on a teenage magazine called *Fabulous*. You had just tip-toed into the charts with your first single 'Baby Let Me Take You Home', and were full of yourselves. You were accompanied by EMI Records' PR Brian Mulligan, who assured me that all the school kids in Newcastle were converts and drawing Animals graphics on their satchels and bag. You didn't look much like new teenage idols to me. Chas Chandler was a great young bear of a man who looked self-conscious under a pudding basin haircut which was presumably supposed to be 'Beatleish', and his bulk shut the sun out when he moved through my door. Alan Price sounded moody and looked mean, whilst you had the appearance of decent young middleweight, with a face to match. Johnny Steele looked deceptively like a shy young accountant. I was accustomed to eulogising and ghosting disc columns for the likes of screamage idols like Cliff, Adam, Marty and now The Beatles, but you lot were a different kettle of rock and despite your friendly approach were certainly not pretty poster fodder. You had faces that broke the pop mould — male, and more like a gang than a group.

I brooded about what I could do with a bunch of Geordie toughs in a teen magazine, whilst staring at the large, spotless white blotter on my desk which was still a status symbol hung over from the bad old days, when the city types were judged by the size of their office and neatness of the desk. I was a prissy little cub reporter then, and my desk was my altar. You, to my horror, suddenly decided to draw great, swirling, black eyes with a felt tip pen all over my sacred blotter to demonstrate your artistic abilities, and the new group logo which you had designed. My face was a mask of indignation at the effrontery. Chas was swiftly into the absurdity and said, 'Do some big ones so Keith can see it properly, Eric.' I caught his eye, recognised my petty conceit had been spotted and laughter took over.

It was not long before you were hugely successful with a string of million-selling singles around the world like 'House of the Rising Sun', 'Don't Let Me Be Misunderstood', 'Boom Boom', 'Bring It On Home To Me', 'It's My Life', 'Don't Bring Me Down', and the Vietnam conscripts unofficial anthem 'We Gotta Get Out of This Place'. Moreover, you were challenging The Beatles and the Stones by 1966 for chart domination.

I was a journalist on *NME* by now, and did not need persuading to accompany you in your old pink Ford

Galaxy (which was indicative of the love affair you had with anything American) so that I could review your gigs. One memorable evening we wound up at a jam session for veteran blues man John Lee Hooker who was celebrating his 40th Birthday at the Newcastle Club A-Go-Go. Alan had gone missing minutes before a photo call so I stood with my back slightly turned and made all the national newspapers as the fifth Animal.

I also distinguished myself by creating something of a sensation with a young girl I found to dance with. A crowd gathered round, and I thought the attraction was due to my neat jiving. It turned out, however, that the Geordies were actually gathering to pay their last respects to me prior to my death. It was you who fought your way through the throng and gasped in horror when you saw my partner. 'Jesus, you're dead,' you informed me. 'Do you know whose girl that is?'

The beautiful young creature clasped to my chest was unknown to me, but I suggested she seemed like a nice girl. 'Nice?' you gasped, 'Nice! That's not nice, that's Mr Big's girlfriend you have there, and when he comes back from the gents you will have your head nailed to the floor.'

It appeared that 'Mr Big' was Newcastle's answer to Ronnie Kray, and I had transgressed the unwritten law by getting within five miles of his girl. Despite my protest that I had left my brand new Hush Puppies at roadie Tappy Wright's house, I was bundled unceremoniously out of Newcastle on the milk train back to London. 'You don't get out now, you wont have any legs to put in the shoes,' you informed me before I was railroaded home. My best shoes, which Tappy's dad informed him later were the most comfortable he had worn at the pit head, turned up 15 years later — but that's another story.

In the early sixties you were an obsessive fan of the magnificently temperamental Nina Simone, and thus hugely pleased with yourself when your cover version of her composition 'Don't Let Me Be Misunderstood' made the top ten with The Animals. Together with Chas and Hilton we went to see her at Finsbury Park Astoria when she toured the UK that year, and were ushered backstage to meet the great lady. One of Nina's management team came back and informed you that she would like to see you personally, and rather smugly you went into her dressing room for what you fancied would be a cosy *tête à tête*, whilst Chas and Hilton were left to cool their heels outside the door with me. Can you imagine their delight when they heard her erupt all over you like a volcano through the closed dressing room door? 'So *you* are the little honky shit who stole my song,' was just for openers, followed by, 'I suppose you are another of these sanctimonious little white bastards who all think we should fall down on our knees and worship you because you have covered our songs — well let me tell you ...' And so on at great length until you were eventually able to convey that not only were you one of her greatest fans, but would make sure she received every penny of the royalties due to her. Miss Simone was eventually appeased.

Your obsession with 'Americana' was given full vent after the break-up of the original Animals in 1966, and you became a convert to the 'love and peace' brigade, which coincided with the formation of The New Animals who were to get their big break at the Monterey Festival with Jimi Hendrix and The Who. This was my first trip to America, and I flew out with Jimi to find that I was doubled up in a room with you at the then infamous Chelsea hotel in New York. One murder a month was the rumour at the time.

After a night at the The Tin Angel club in the Village with Jimi, where we watched an as yet unknown Ritchie Havens in great form, I was awoken in my room by your return from a party aboard John Bloom's yacht in New York harbour. You were plainly chemically assisted and blithering about the wonderful lights you could see everywhere and how the whole world was going to be re-invented by Timothy Leary and LSD. Peace and love was in the air and Scot McKenzie was number one in the singles charts with 'If You Go To San Francisco — Wear Some Flowers in Your Hair' whilst The Beatles had just released *Sergeant Pepper's Lonely Hearts Club Band*, so it was difficult not to be affected by the flower children and the beautiful people's pipe dreams. 'Everything is going to change,' you informed me that night 'Everything — the long hairs are taking over.' Tell that to the guys with the mohair suits and the big cigars still in control in the nineties.

For a short while it almost looked as if giving 'peace a chance' might succeed, and you chalked up your first major self-written hit with 'San Franciscan Nights' and 'Monterey' following your appearance on that memorable first open air Festival in Monterey. Wearing your psychedelic gear we strolled around the concert grounds with a new young hopeful called Janis Joplin, and listened to Otis Redding with a pale Brian Jones in his chiffon and lace looking 'like a ghost leaving a seance,' as Keith Richards once described him.

But then The Beatles disbanded, and their shop and the Apple Company were in ruins, while bean-counters like Allen Klein were taking care of business again — the hippy dream was dead. The bread-heads were in charge once more, The New Animals had disbanded, and you were cajoled into the first reunion with the 'originals' at Newcastle City Hall, still disconsolately clinging to your kaftan and beads. 'The New Animals broke up just the way the old Animals did,' you revealed sadly during an interview I did for BBC's *Scene and Heard* radio programme. 'Their egos exploded.'

At the reunion concert at Newcastle City Hall you were brought crashing back to earth from 'The Beautiful People' by no less than the unbeautiful 'Mr Big' who, unamused at his not being granted VIP status at the stage door, demanded to see you. Dressed in your kaftan and beads, you rather unwisely decided you would go and attempt to reason with the uncrowned King of Newcastle and explain that there were no backstage passes and he should try some 'positive vibes'. Having attempted to convey the message of peace and love though a gap in the stage door it appears you then assaulted Mr Big's knuckles with your nose and came back to the dressing room having broken your beads and bleeding copiously.

Alan Price, who had been on the wagon, promptly fell off it and poured a bottle of vodka down himself at the sound check, whilst Chas pounded his chest on stage, suggesting that what this band needed was someone to take charge, namely him. Hilton, who had lately become a Buddhist, was attempting to meditate himself somewhere else — anywhere else, and the sane John Steel was clutching his head in his hands over his drum kit mumbling , 'It's just the same — it's just the same.' Spinal Tap had nothing on The Animals.

Nothing daunted by the demise of Peace and Love, you returned to America to reinvent yourself again and found a wonderful collection of talented black musicians which you threw together under the ironic name of War. 'I don't just want to be known as a dirty old blues singer all my life,' you declared. 'War is not in opposition to the peace movement, it embraces love and peace because so does war. I chose the name because I have always been at war with myself. People seem to get some satisfaction out of watching me tear myself apart and I have always felt that if I ever do find peace of mind I won't be of interest to anyone.'

War, in fact, proved to be as brilliant a band as you could wish to hear and put you back to the US top ten with 'Spill the Wine' in the seventies, and your UK tour had *NME* writers like the highly respected Roy Carr rhapsodising about it being the best live band in the world.

There was a monumental confrontation at one gig where Elton John and War were on the same bill which resulted in a flaming row between you. 'It was just one of those things,' you told me with a grin after the show. 'Elton had the option to go on before us, and maybe it was unfortunate that our first number lasted 55 minutes so he was a little late coming on.'

The other great obsession in your life has been films, and it is one area you have never really cracked. You also had an endearing but dangerous tendency to attack and debunk any kind of establishment authority without considering the possibility that they may be offering you a useful platform. Chas Chandler told me a classic tale of a formal dinner party he had been invited to at the mansion of a top Hollywood producer, and he rang you to see if you would like to join him at the table with some of the film moguls who might make useful contacts for you. During dinner you apparently became miffed at being sidelined as the conversation soared into the lofty realms of American politics, investments and high finance, peppered with the usual pomposity. Eventually the mogul turned to you and, in an attempt to bring you into the conversation, asked, 'Your friend Mr Chandler tells me you have some very interesting cinematic plans, Mr Burdon. Perhaps you would like to enlighten us about them?'

You leapt kamikaze-like into the gap. 'Well I got this idea about this guy who has the biggest donger in the world, and he meets this girl who has the biggest cunt in the world and they ...' There then followed an outrageous exposition which would have graced any major porno flick in the world and produced a stunned silence from the host and his family lasting some minutes before he, embarrassed, moved on to other matters.

The death of your friend Jimi Hendrix, which you were brought into by association after his girlfriend phoned you the night of his death to request help when she could not wake him, seemed to unhinge you for a while, and you made emotional statements on TV about 'carrying on his torch for him'.

The years rolled by, and as War's initial promise disappeared, so you formed other bands and kept the fires stoked in America and Germany whilst occasionally staying in England with friends like me and Zoot Money, whom you knew from the days when he played with his own band and later with The New Animals. Zoot tells a defining story of your life cycle when he found you stoned, frantically rooting through drawers and under cushions in his Fulham home looking for a 'critical' memo you had written to yourself on what you must do with your life on your return to the US that morning. After your departure, Zoot finally found the lost memo under his coffee pot in the kitchen. It read simply, 'Sack Manager. Get Divorce. Fire solicitor. Form new band and hire new accountant.' Zoot was somewhat at a loss to understand how you could possibly forget the five guiding principles which seemed to have governed your entire life.

By l983 your career had hit another lull, and yet another reunion with the original Animals loomed in which I was to pay an active part as 'referee' and publicist for a world tour. Everything was agreed and set according to Alan Price and Chas Chandler who had invited me down as a 'hostage' for your first meet at Mr Price's country house. You eventually arrived three hours later in your typical 'bull in a china shop' mode and proceeded to take on Alan over arrangements and Chas over whether he could still play bass. 'What you guys don't realise is that it is my neck on the line out there,' you said. 'I am the one out in front and it is me the critics will murder if we sound like the bunch of amateurs we were in the Sixties playing all the same old crap again.'

In an attempt to placate you, Chas enquired what new numbers you would like to play, and you took off your army knapsack (you always seem to have an army knapsack) and drop-kicked it into his face across the lounge. 'Help yourself,' you suggested graciously. 'I've been carrying the crap around for the past ten years.' I made my excuses and left — promising to return when the smoke had cleared.

Amazingly things were worked out on the basis that everyone employed their own manager to represent their own interests, and it proved so contentious that the tour disintegrated prior to Japan, just as The Animals were about to go into profit. By this time, Chas threatened your manager he would kill him and after a few beers you informed Alan Price you were taking out a 'contract' on Chas' family, which he thoughtfully passed on to Chas. Hilton 'Om'-ed in true Buddhist style and John Steel put his fingers in his ears and hummed loudly.

Initially I had taken the decision as your PR that the

only way to get national coverage up front was to make a virtue of the acrimony and promote the tour as a glorified 'punch up'. The national press love a good fight, and you started the ball rolling in no mean fashion by summing up your touring party to the *News of the World* as a 'forced march', although it might be mentioned that you were the only one who protested about drummer John Steel and guitarist Hilton Valentine being made junior and unequal partners in the venture. 'Alan and Chas are right-wing bullies only in it for the money,' you declared. 'Hilton Valentine has become one of the great unemployed Buddhists of our time, and John Steel is a bleeding-heart liberal conservative living with his beautiful wife and his beautiful daughter in his beautiful house in Northumberland. I am considered one of the great unwashed.'

Chas Chandler responded, 'Eric is a dreamer and he has always been a dreamer with out any common sense. He was the kind of idiot art student in the early days who wanted to throw everything away for art's sake and follow his heart. That is why is always broke.'

Somehow, through all the retakes, remakes and reunions, after you have been beaten to your knees, as your bands fold, you arise Custer-like from the dust and make another stand with yet another Eric Burdon Band and hit the trail. Last man standing. The last we saw of you on TV here was almost a year ago, with a full-length grey pony tail on your hands and knees lighting a candle for Linda Eastman on her sad death in LA.

If ever a man with a great blues voice and a big heart was able lyrically to convey the pain and confusion of his past life it is you. You are one of the few rock writers I can think of who is capable of conjuring up the spirit of your times in an historical cameo, as you did beautifully with 'San Franciscan Nights' and 'Monterey'. You captured that whole hippy, beautiful people, flower in your hair, peace and love period. You should tell the tale of your life in music. You should write a biographical-historical CD now. There are those white musicians playing the blues who have never had them, but that could not be said of you, in your scarred rock and roll lifetime. Always a trier; always a dreamer; always a brave heart, if sometimes a tad wrong-headed.

Dirty old blues singers can rool OK.

Keith

VAN
MORRISON

VAN MORRISON

A LEGEND IN HIS OWN GUINNESS

Dear Van,

What can I say? What a talent. What a singer. What a songwriter. What a pain in the arse. I think it would be impossible to find anyone as contrary or cussed as you, despite your being one of the most respected, original and eclectic musical talents I have represented as a press agent.

More mad Irish poet than pop star. More inspired jazz musician than rock star. More a visionary than an icon and more talented than tortured. You have that unique feeling for song that seems to be ripped out of your soul and emerges like a painful paean. You can comfortably communicate with the best of the jazz, rock, soul or blues artistes musically, but God help the reporter who gets his facts wrong, or dares to ask 'How are you?'

'Down all the Days', you seem to have lost patience and the desire to communicate with the media, and even on occasion the audience, unless it was through your music. Conversation became cheap and the music became the means by which you made meaningful contact. Small talk is not something you have ever considered useful or constructive.

I must say in defence of your dismissive manner that you were never one of the those artistes who hypocritically used journalists in the early days and then refused co-operation later. You were a bolshy bugger from round one in the early sixties, and employed all the charm of a toad and the charisma of a dialling tone to fend off anyone who wanted to know what your favourite colour was and if you had any hobbies.

My first confrontation with you (you like confrontations and use them to assess people) was way back in 1964 when I elected to interview your band Them for the *NME* where I was a journalist. You had just entered the charts with 'Here Comes The Night'.

I liked rock and roll mavericks, and I was intrigued by the story I had heard about you appearing on stage in Belfast in front of a bunch of none-too-appreciative teddy boys. Armed with a book upon which you fixed your gaze, you addressed them. 'To wank or not to wank, that is the question.' You then enquired how many 'wankers' there were in the audience. Eric Burdon had also spoken highly of you, although he did add the codicil: 'Completely nuts of course'. Nothing prepared me for the real thing.

The fact that you were being represented at the time by the same man who managed other traditional Irish talents like Ruby Murray (the fifties' answer to Vera Lynn) and The Bachelors, who were candy-sugar music for Mum, Dad and Auntie Doris seemed an anachronism. However, nothing daunted, I arrived at your rehearsal studio and got the traditional Van Morrison elbow in the face with 'I'm too busy to talk to you — go and talk to the boys.' You gestured towards an unlikely looking bunch of surly miscreants and guitarist Billy Harrison.

'I really wanted to talk to *you*,' I explained. 'And I do have another interview with Mick Jagger in an hour,' I added for the sake of effect. 'Fuck Mick Jagger,' you responded smoothly, and went back into discussions with Bert Berns who had written your hit and seemed hugely amused by the exchange. I was miffed and went off to talk with the surly Mr Harrison who was busy excavating his fingernails with a jack knife, which he continued to do while I talked to him.

The band proved as inarticulate and uncooperative as yourself, and so I decided to get my own back by writing up the monosyllabic responses, conveying the general atmosphere of hostility and bad manners. It made a controversial piece in the *NME* to the extent that I was hauled in by my Editor Maurice Kinn with whom your manager, unbeknown to me, was close friends and asked not to embarrass him again. I affirmed I had no intention of interviewing you again so this was unlikely. I could sense that my Editor was secretly amused by the whole incident but trying not to show it.

It seemed that a part of your dissatisfaction and disillusionment with Them came from the covert use of session guitarists, like Jimmy Page, who were introduced on to your sessions because the group were not considered experienced enough by Decca Records and Dick Rowe (the man who infamously turned down the Beatles but redeemed himself by signing the Rolling Stones). The albums *Them* and *Them Again* were thus almost disowned by you.

The years span round, classic songs like 'Gloria' and 'Brown Eyed Girl' came and went and you disappeared on a quest of some kind to the West Coast of America. In 1966, I was out in Hollywood doing an interview with the bearded Jim Morrison who, although a little precious, was extremely likeable, and waxed lyrical about your appearances out there and the hard drinking down at the Whisky-A-Go-Go.

Morrison J lavishly credited you and Eric Burdon with teaching him 'how not to drink', and you were the only two he trusted to get him home. He told me that he believed you had more talent in your 'pinky' than he had in his whole body. He gave me your telephone number, but I decided not to repeat my previous experience — a decision I regretted later as subsequent albums like *Astral Weeks*, *Moondance*, and *Tupelo Honey* were light years ahead of anything attempted by most other artistes.

After your divorce from Janet Planet (a name to conjure with) after a five-year marriage, and your disillusionment with your country retreat in America, you seemed to return to your normal, paranoid, lugubrious self as you picked up pain like most of us do colds. You went from brooding through Colin Wilson, to searching for the meaning of life in a grain of sand with William Blake, and flirted with 'clearing' yourself in Scientology. Your album *Inarticulate Speech* was dedicated to the ex-science fiction writer L Ron Hubbard who had founded the Scientology cult.

My friend Moria Bellas who was MD at WEA Records in the eighties had encountered the familiar problem of your being unable to relate to their current press office. You had issued an edict, for example, that any photographer accompanying a journalist could shoot one frame. She was looking for someone to take on the poison chalice. I agreed a six-month contract to do your press, with the proviso that I was paid up front and in advance.

To illustrate the problems I was likely to encounter with you the record company told me a story circulating at the time. In desperation to get you to do just one interview for the forthcoming tour, they had flown your childhood friend Sam Woodburn to LA (he whom you had immortalised on 'Cleaning Windows') all expenses paid. He was now working for a respected Irish newspaper.

The story goes that Sam arrived at your home on the West Coast during a heatwave, direct from the airport, and collapsed into a chair in your house. You, however, decided it was time to go for a drink at the local bar — which was strange because at the time you did not drink. Down the hill from the house you stomped, which was some few miles. Sam, who was not tee-total, but who was overweight, just had time to stop sweating profusely and down one beer before you decided, like the Grand Old Duke of York, to march him back up the hill again.

Everything seemed to be going reasonably well until you arrived back at the house and Sam made his move. He had decided that the best course of action was to get the interview over swiftly so that you could both relax and spend the next few days having a good time and reminiscing about the good old days. It was then that he made his big mistake by producing a pocket tape recorder, placing it on a table and asking you a question.

'This is a trick,' you apparently responded. 'You are trying to trick me and I will not have it.' In vain your old chum tried to convince you he was just a friend from the old days who was now a journalist. You sniffed conspiracy — you would probably consider it a conspiracy if someone asked you the time. He went home and the interview was never completed.

My first meet with you as your press agent was set up at The Royal Garden Hotel in London, where I found you in the restaurant, obliviously flossing your teeth whilst the more genteel diners looked on with obvious distaste. You carried on your dental toilet as we talked and thankfully you seem to have completely forgotten me from our confrontation in the sixties.

'My problem,' you mumbled mid-floss, sawing at your molars with a length of tooth flax, 'is that I do not consider the media have any right to any kind of insight into my private life. Now I have my *Wavelength* album to promote, and an Irish tour. I will talk music and I will only talk music if the questions are intelligent and appropriate. I also hate all the photographs that my record company have on file.'

I arranged a new photo session with Brian Aris, who was renowned for being able to make Andrew Lloyd Webber look like Mel Gibson, and who also had a great deal of patience with difficult artistes. It was the first of many sessions I did with the talented Brian over the years and I was eager to make his acquaintance and that nothing should go terribly wrong. You agreed to the session and then typically turned up three hours late. Eventually you arrived, clutching your tenor sax and grumbling something about having problems with the dentist. You had been in the outer studio with Brian no more than ten minutes when there was a crashing of tripods and you barged your way out announcing with great charm in front of the lady assistant that you had 'done with all that fucking posing years ago'. It was confrontation time.

'Van, this is the best photographer in the business, and he is capable of taking a shot which even if reduced to a column inch will still make you look good and be reproducable and acceptable in any newspaper, magazine or periodical across the world.' I explained to you. 'If that is not what you want, you must put up with them using the same old publicity shots you hate.'

Out came your finger which you jabbed theatrically

in front of my face: 'I am paying you to say "No, No, No,"' you exploded.

'You are paying me nothing,' I responded. 'I have already been paid because I know how difficult you can be. But if that is really what you want, I suggest you simply employ an answering machine, a secretary or even better, train a parrot.'

You seemed taken aback by this and muttered something to the effect that you would think about that and shouldered your way out again. I was left apologising to Brian who had never had a ten-minute photo-session before, and thankfully was more bewildered than angry.

Three days later at my home the phone rang and it proved to be Yourself. You announced melodramatically that you had been thinking over what I said. 'I think you know what you're talking about,' you said magnanimously. 'What precisely do you want me to do?' I suggest just three interviews. One for the music press with Tony Stewart of the *NME*, John Tobler for the syndicated radio and The Press Association. You agreed that we should accompany you on your Irish dates. In Belfast there was one surreal moment with your band when we returned to the hotel after a concert, in the early hours of morning. We were sitting around the reception area in front of the elevators having a nightcap, when the unmistakeable figure of Hughie Green, the elderly TV presenter, walked boldly through the doors to the lift with an attractive young blonde on his arm.

There was an ominous silence as your band surveyed this apparition, and then an inspired intervention by guitarist Bobby Tench who broke the silence by leaping to his feet pointing accusingly at the closing doors of the lift and shouting in mimicry of

Hughie's famous catchphrase, 'Tonight, Hugh Greene, for you ... Opportunity Knocks!' I think there was even a ghost of a smile on your lips, but mostly you seemed to have done with smiling after your skiffling days with The Sputniks and the Irish showband The Monarchs.

These were the first concerts you had played in Ireland for nearly 12 years, and at first the interviews went well. Then we hit Belfast where you had trouble with a heckler in the audience and returned to the hotel, in a less than receptive mood, where you entered your darkened room from which you had the TV and other extraneous furniture other than the bed removed. I never found out why, but I feel sure there was a major conspiracy involving furniture.

Later when I approached you in the restaurant to commiserate over the heckler you shrugged and asked where the *NME* journalist was, and that you wanted to film the interview with him for the documentary of the tour you were making. I checked with Tony and he asked suspiciously, 'Am I being set up here?' Paranoia unlimited. I promised to be present at the interview being conducted in your suite and perched on a bed as the cameras rolled. This exchange was one of your gems.

'Right,' said Tony. 'Now tell me, Van, when you were recording *Veedon Fleece* was it ...'

'Ahm not answering personal questions,' you cut in.

'No, Van, you see that is a question about your music,' said a bewildered Tony Stewart.

'Well I'm not answering it.'

'If you do not want to answer questions why are you doing the interview?'

'Now I have nothing against you personally, but behind you there is a man who is trying to sell papers on my name.'

'Then why are we doing this?'

'Because if people see this film and understand just what it is that I am trying to say, then it has been worthwhile my doing this interview.'

'Well, what is it that you are trying to say?'

'I don't like doing interviews.'

QED

Amazingly you kept up this tortuous performance for almost an hour and kept returning to your original point which most of us would have found self-evident. It fortunately provided Tony Stewart with a front-page story for *NME* and an eccentric three-page feature inside which added further fuel to the legend.

You are not an artiste who could never be accused of being vain about your appearance, and 'image' and 'product' are forbidden words, but sometimes your scruffy sense can work against you. There was one delightful moment at an after-show party to which you were invited after you had headlined an outdoor festival. The promoter wisely couched it in terms that they would be delighted to see you but understood if you preferred your privacy.

'The party will be in the big barn behind the stage and will go on all night and into the morning,' said the promoter. 'So come any time if you feel like it.' You grunted acknowledgement, but no one expected you to grace the occasion.

It was 3 a.m. when almost everyone had departed but a few hardy souls, still holding up the bar, when there came a banging on the barn door to reveal you in a flat cap, anorak and cord trousers with frost on your nose. The massive security man on duty looked upon you for a few seconds and then bellowed to the remaining guests inside, 'Anyone order a mini-cab?' Strangely, I think you might have liked that.

There were not many laughs during the few months

that I represented you, although I can remember one bizarre moment in a restaurant on the border between Dublin and Belfast when we were ordering a meal together. It was just the two of us across a table and I found myself completely unable to fathom the waitress' Northern Irish accent. I was trying not to embarrass her, not to embarrass myself, and not to embarrass you over my inability to grasp what she was saying. My vigorous nodding only produced a torrent from the colleen of what sounded to me more like Martian. As things wound to a totally absurd level, with you acting as interpreter, I could see you suppressing laughter, which turned to hysterical tears, which of course started me and suddenly we both 'corpsed' and became unable, to the poor girl's utter confusion, to order anything. It was the only occasion I ever felt an empathy with you personally.

I only ran into you once after my stint umpiring your war with the press, and that was a few years ago in Ronnie Scott's club in London when we were there to see the Charlie Watts Big Band. I crossed the club to say hello and to congratulate you on a series you had recently presented on Irish poets for TV. 'It was beautifully shot and your insights were illuminating,' I ventured.

'Yeah,' you said looking through me as though I were a Vulcan.

The truth is that you are an impossible man, but were you not wrestling with demons you would probably not be the massive talent you are.

Live long and prosper, Van.

Keith

BRIAN
WILSON

Keith with the *Beach Boys* after Brian Wilson stopped touring.

BRIAN WILSON

THE HAUNTED BEACH BOY

Dear Brian,

If ever an artiste suffered for his music and his sanity it is you, and those in any doubt need only check out any recent photograph to see the haunted face of a Beach Boy who has tottered on the brink of the abyss and fallen backwards into the stark reality which has already deprived you of your younger brothers Dennis and Carl. You, my friend, are some survivor.

In my three year tenure of representing the Beach Boys press during the release of the albums *20/20* and *Sunflower*, I only met you twice, and even then under bizarre circumstances. You are one of the few true popular music geniuses, even if you did spend much of those early years in LA in a stupor with your toes in a sand box, carefully avoiding the doggie pooh. You worked in hope of catching another wave of inspiration at your grand piano which would supersede *Pet Sounds*, or hid inside your plastic pyramid where other good vibes were suppose to be attracted.

My first meeting with you was conducted from the vantage point of being a rock journalist for *NME*, and I had a few words with you at your lunchtime press reception in the early sixties when you were photographed outside EMI House in Manchester Square, looking hugely embarrassed whilst clasping some wooden planks under one arm with the other Beach Boys for a photo call. There were no surf boards available in London at the time. You did not surf.

Privately you confessed to loving the West Coast beach lifestyle, but were afraid of the sea so clinging to a piece of driftwood was somehow quite appropriate. I was not a surf music fan and had yet to become converted to the group. Thanks to Rolling Stones manager Andrew Loog Oldham I did become the first journalist to hear *Pet Sounds* in the UK and recognise it as a rock classic far removed from your early teen-surfing safaris.

It must have hurt you deeply when the American critics and the US public initially failed to separate the new music from the old image, and only grudgingly bestowed any real artistic appreciation upon the album years later. Beach Boys apparently were supposed to stick to beach music in the US in the sixties and that blinkered outlook was not without credence even amongst your group at the time, and was certainly affirmed by your early manager, father and Philistine — Murry Wilson.

I was doing an interview in late 1965 with Jagger at Immediate Records in New Oxford Street. He became an early Beach Boys convert when Andrew Oldham went into overdrive about the *Pet Sounds* album he had somehow smuggled back to the UK in the form of an acetate. He brainwashed me over its merits in his office in New Oxford Street. 'Listen to this,' raved Andrew, recently returned from the US and tweaked up the volume another few notches as the exquisite sounds of 'I Just Wasn't Made For these Times' blasted his employees homeward. 'Brian has only got one good ear — one good ear,' he informed me, raising his eyebrows heavenward. 'The man is a fucking master-class in pop music — now listen to how he has layered this track. A fruit cake — but what a genius!

'Brian has got ten speakers on one wall and one on the other to balance his hearing deficiency. Some fucking deficiency — most of the critics can't hear what he is doing with two *good* ears.' In those days 'The Loog' was in tune with almost everything worthwhile happening in pop music, and after an hour of this sort of rant I began to realise he was right again, and this album was more than something special. The first Beach Boys album to be recorded in stereo was *Friends* years later, and this was alleged to be your favourite.

Andrew fixed me up with an exclusive interview with Bruce Johnston who had become the new Beach Boy, brought in by the band when you could no longer contain the stresses and strains of touring. Bruce flew into London days later with a final mix of *Pet Sounds* and went through it track by track with me at the Savoy. I went into rave mode in my *NME* review and became a Beach Boys fan from that moment on.

1966 was a golden year when 'Good Vibrations' hit number one in the charts and the Beach Boys flew into Heathrow airport to an hysterical screamage reception. I was there to meet you, and was disappointed to discover that you had not made the trip even in a non-playing capacity but, together with two young girls who appeared to be welded to his legs, I wound up in a limo back to the Hilton with your brother Dennis. He was your drummer and all good looks, charm and bullshit, but he did his bit when it came to promotion.

It was from Dennis that I learnt the story of how the Beach Boys had been on tour and returned to find a virtually completed album on which you had written, sung, played and produced everything, even over-dubbing the harmonies. That was *Pet Sounds*. There were naturally those in the band who were somewhat miffed at this solo flight, including cousin Mike Love who was also unsure about a surfing-group having inherited an album called *Pet Sounds* on which they were virtually non-participants.

A few compromises were made, but what was a virtuoso performance from you became the Beach Boys next album with one of the most twee sleeves in the history of pop, depicting the band feeding a variety of beasts as though you were in Pets Corner of the LA Zoo.

On the drive from the airport, Dennis divested himself of the two groupies and went into PR mode over you: 'Brian is not just our songwriter — Brian *is* the fucking Beach Boys,' Dennis told me proudly. He was fiercely loyal in public about you. 'What we do is to get out there on the road and try and polish the diamonds Brian has cut in the studio. We can make them sparkle in the open and we do it better than anyone else, but it would be even better with Brian. Sometimes I feel like the Beatles without John Lennon.'

Your late younger brother Carl, always a gentle soul, was more sanguine when I spoke to him about your importance to the Beach Boys later at the Hilton. 'We all know how important Brian is to our success as a songwriter,' said Carl, 'But you must also bear in mind that this has been a group-family effort now for almost a decade, and without the energy and enthusiasm of people like Mike Love and Al Jardine, and their musical contributions, we would not have got this far as a group. Brian's music would not be heard live or performed because he will not tour so we provide that platform and promotion.

'The Beach Boys are no more a one-man band than are the Beatles or the Stones. We are a group and we all contribute something special, even Dennis,' added Carl with a sideways glance, as your brother disappeared into an adjacent bedroom to give an 'exclusive' to another female admirer.

Carl was a much underestimated force and with his cool head and gentle but firm guidance he slowly became a rock on which the survival of the group as a live force was founded in your absence, for decades to come. Mike was a driving force, and a showman on-stage, but it was Carl's developing vocal authority and composing ability which made the group without you secure live. Carl was the group member who sat quietly with Glen Campbell when the rest of the group had given up hope of ever working again without you on tour, and taught him enough numbers in a few hours to enable him to substitute for you on-stage before he went solo to be replaced by Bruce.

Your guitarist, Al Jardine, was an amusing enigma as he seemed on the surface to adopt an anything-for-a-peaceful-life pose, but I suspected that someone who had been a junior shotput champion would not be pushed too far. I remember going out shopping with him once in Holland and he bought a boomerang to take home to LA for his kids.

'Why not?' he shrugged. 'I have to buy something, and you can't lose these.'

Al tended to be a perfectionist with his guitar tuning, and after the Hammersmith show in London he passed me perspiring in the wings and grinned, 'Well, that's the guitar tuned — now for the show.'

The main problem with your late brother Dennis was that he was not very perceptive. Or as Mike once put it to me so succinctly — 'The first thing you have to understand about Dennis is that he does not understand.' If he had been a little brighter, he might have seen some of the dangers of living life permanently on the edge and been able to distinguish between a shaman and a charlatan. In 1967 he was the first to meet the giggling guru Maharishi Mahesh Yogi who had advised him, 'Live your life to the fullest,' which was all Dennis needed to encourage him into introducing him to you all as a sage.

The guiding principles of meditation and mantras stayed with the other Beach Boys long after the Beatles gave up the ghost and Ringo returned from his Indian ashram with the damning news that 'It was a bit like Butlins.' I can remember several flights with the boys when there was time out called for a 'meditation break' up front in the plane.

Meanwhile, back in LA, you were casting the *I Ching* about and listening to the crystal huggers and astrologers while toying with religious cults like Subud which caused Jim McGuinn of the Byrds to change his name to Roger and back again. You seemed to be swimming though a sea of drugs, and I fear that having suffered childhood trauma it only fuelled your fantasies and paranoia.

Dennis suffered from his own delusion, and there was a chilling moment when I went on tour with the Beach Boys in 1968 to review a concert in Paris. Dennis explained to me one night over dinner in a restaurant on the Left Bank about this fascinating 'wizard' he had found. He had turned over his home in LA to him and his hippie entourage. There were just the two of us and I shall never forget the shudder that went down my back when he told me about them in subdued tones, leaning forwards and pushing his smiling face into mine, 'You

NO MORE MR NICE GUY

see, Keith, one minute he is Jesus,' and he turned away. When he turned back I can only say that his face had changed to demonic proportions and he screamed, 'and the next he is the Devil!'

I am sure it sounds melodramatic in retrospect to you, but your young brother scared the hell out of me, literally raising the hairs on the back of my neck. I will never forget the first time I heard him utter the name of 'Charles Manson', who was later convicted of the horrific murder of Hollywood actress Sharon Tate.

Although Manson used your studio to record, somehow you seemed to avoid contact with either the Maharishi or Charlie and his crazed cult. Great evasive technique as usual. Manson almost bankrupted Dennis and stole his Ferrari before he came to his senses, and he evicted him shortly before the murder. At that time Manson was looking for him with a hunting knife.

Dennis, as you know, was a 'searcher' and a womaniser, but he too had been traumatised by some appalling discipline at the hands of your bombastic father whom he told me had burnt his hands on one occasion for playing with matches in the house as a kid, and attempted to beat the devil out of him with a belt and piece of two by four on other occasions. You suffered at his hands to the extent that one blow even allegedly contributed to your partial deafness. There was a falling out between you and Carl in the nineties when you refused to attend your father's funeral, but I can only say your absence was sadly understandable.

When I first met Murry who accompanied the Boys on a tour of Europe in the early seventies, I gained some understanding of your childhood problems. He was chauvinistic, domineering and insensitive to the extent that one would visibly cringe with embarrassment as you witnessed him trying to stuff dollar bills down an air-stewardess blouse as he attempted to make his presence felt as the 'The Big I Was' on the airplane. Murry was simply a big-head and bully.

The best that can be said of him was that his own limited musical ambition having been thwarted, he saw an opportunity vicariously to rectify his comparative musical failure by managing you and turning you into teenage idols on the back of the surfing craze. His failure to see that you had matured into something far more complex and poetic was as inevitable as was his removal.

In 1970 I had the misfortune to be included on the infamous 'Brinzley Schwartz Hype' to America which consisted of a jet-load of journalists and the like being flown out to New York on a privately-hired old prop-driven Stratocruiser to see the group play, and back the same night. Suffice to say that the plane leaked hydraulic fuel all over the runway at Heathrow and came down in Shannon for a refit before eventually limping into New York with two propellers feathered. One more out of action and we were informed by the captain, who bore a passing resemblance to James Stewart, that we would 'go down like a fucking wardrobe'. We were just in time to make the Filimore East to witness the group waving to us all and thanking us for being a wonderful audience.

I decided that no way was I getting back on that death-trap, and placed a call to you in LA to see if you were interested in paying my internal air fare so that I could interview you for *NME*. I was promised that I could see you, although you were reportedly in ill health again and there were stories of you having dug a grave in your back garden and attempting to jump off your garage into it.

Bruce Johnston turned up at the Beverly Rodeo

Hotel on Sunset Strip to meet me, and put me in the picture about your latest predicament with Capitol records who had withdrawn *Pet Sounds*, *Friends*, *Smiley Smile* and *Wild Honey* and re-promoted all the early surfing material. I am sure you remember the never-ending battle with the American record company to recognise you for something other than surfing anthems.

'Brian has been fighting this antiquated image for years in America,' raged Bruce. 'It's like recognising the Beatles for 'I Want To Hold Your Hand' and then promoting them at that level for the rest of their musical lives. We have been pioneers in so many fields that no one has credited us for. Brother Records was the first rock artiste-owned label. We were the first to use a moog synthesizer and we are the biggest-selling American group in record history but they still will not take us seriously here in the US.'

Would a change of name help, I suggested, little knowing that at one time Mike had half-seriously suggested terminating the name to 'Beach'.

'A change of name is a nowhere game' responded Dennis later. 'We have all spent a decade building up the brand name and our reputations are linked to albums like *Wild Honey* and *Smiley Smile*, of which the Beach Boys are justly proud.'

It was Dennis who conspiratorially agreed, at my request, to take me to see you. The following day we motored out to a health restaurant called The Radiant Radish in which I was informed you had an interest. We parked head-on to a large window through which I could see the shopping alleys inside, when suddenly from around the corner shuffled this huge, bloated figure in what looked like a dressing gown and slippers. 'There,' said Dennis excitedly pointing, 'There he is.'

You began taking tins and bottles of honey from a shelf.

'Great,' I said, 'let's go and talk to him.' I opened the door of the car. Dennis leaned over and slammed it shut.

'Talk?' said Dennis. 'You don't "talk" to Brian. No one "talks" to Brian. I thought you just wanted to "see" him.' I felt like I had just visited the polar bear in his cage at the LA zoo as we drove away. It was not a good feeling.

Crazy stories about your behaviour were in abundance in those days, and a few months later, when I interviewed your first wife Marilyn for her own album *Spring*, she confirmed a few strange stories but made a plea for more tolerance.

'Why is it that everyone here thinks of Brian as some kind of freak?' she queried. 'I know the piano in the sandbox must seem sort of weird, but haven't you ever fancied just playing in the sand again like a kid. He liked the feel of the sand between his toes and he wrote 'Heroes and Villains' like that, and he wrote 'Surfin' Down the Swanee River' for my album.

'People should just realise that Brian is the greatest singer in the world — he truly *means* what he sings. For example, if Brian sang "The lamp is coming off the wall," then it would seem as though the lamp really were coming off the wall.'

Then of course there were the strange stories of the 'Lost Album' which started out as 'Mrs O'Leary's Cow'. This was the animal said to have accidentally started the the Great Chicago Fire of 1871, and around which the famous lost *Fire* album was built. Marilyn confirmed that she purchased firemen's helmets for everyone to wear in the studio, where at one time you had fires in buckets so that everyone could smell the smoke and pick up the 'elemental vibes'.

The *Fire* album was aborted when freak fires broke out simultaneously all over LA and you decided Nero-like it was some kind of witchcraft which was connected to your composing. You destroyed all the tapes, although Marilyn always held to a theory they still exist.

'Heroes and Villains' was to have been the masterpiece which would eclipse even 'Good Vibrations' and *Pet Sounds*, and I had been played at least three versions at Mike Love's house in Hollywood, including one which ran for six-and-a-half minutes. After having brooded on this song for nearly two years, you announced that your astrologist had deemed the time was now propitious to release it at 3 a.m. one morning in LA and promptly hired five Rolls Royces to appear, Messiah-like, at the local radio station, bearing the Holy Grail of your latest masterpiece so that the DJ on air at the time would have a world exclusive of the song the world was waiting for.

Unfortunately, the DJ on duty at KHJ was not one of your greatest fans, and failed to appreciate the honour he was being afforded by you personally. He explained he could not play anything that was not on the play list. The radio controller was eventually woken and instructed his minion to 'Play it, you idiot,' but the rejection had broken the spell.

Not only had your work not been received with proper deference, but sadly the classic single only scraped into the top ten. You were mortified that something you had worked on for nearly two years should be so discourteously received and went once more into retreat.

Gradually, your health has improved, notably under the svengali-like influence of psychiatrist Eugene Landy. You were able to rejoin the group on-stage, and produce your own solo albums, and recognition long overdue came from august areas like the White House, where the Beach Boys were invited to play at presidential inauguration ceremonies as though you were the living embodiment of the American dream.

For a few years in the seventies, you incongruously added two South African musicians in the shape of Ricky Fattar (drums) and Blondie Chaplin (guitar), and Bruce Johnston quit after a row with your management only to be reclaimed in the eighties. In 1988 you make a solo album *Brian Wilson* and another in 1995 called *I Just Wasn't Made For These Times*, but nothing ever quite recaptured the glory days of the late sixties. Dennis tragically drowned in 1983, and Carl lost his battle with cancer in 1999.

Whither the Beach Boys now? One thing is certain — you will carry on bearing your own personal cross and writing and singing some of the most beautiful and often unappreciated love songs. I sincerely hope you find happiness and peace of mind, because no one I have worked for has paid a price quite like you.

Surf's up

Keith

PAUL
WELLER

Paul Weller (centre)
with *Jam* colleagues
Rick Buckler (left) and
Bruce Foxton (right).

PAUL WELLER

ANGRY YOUNG JAM

Dear Paul,

You were a typical uptight, monosyllabic, suspicious, belligerent little nineteen-year-old punk when I met you in the seventies 'New Wave' era. I liked you instantly. You and The Jam actually came across more like a bunch of scruffy grammar-school kids than anarchists. Sullen, moody, angry with the Establishment, non-communicative and desperately looking for a new way to express it.

You found your way out with the guitar, taking on the Establishment and the conflict that youth will always empathise with. It was *us* against *them*, again. You had passion and compassion — and you understood the frustrations of your own generation and the mess mine had helped make. You reminded me emotionally of the young Pete Townshend.

> *Even at school I felt quite sure*
> *that one day I would be on top*
> *And look down upon the map*
> *of teachers who said I'd be nothing*

You made me come over all Mod and want to dust the rust off my old Lambretta 125 and start polishing the mirrors — but that was first time around, and this was your time. I probably had more in common generation-wise with your old man John Weller who was your manager.

John was silver-haired, broad-chested, his white shirt sleeves rolled up ready to wallpaper your living room in double-quick time. How he did not get eaten alive in the music business I will never understand. He might not have understood the tricks of my trade but he was straight as a dye and honest as the day is long. I liked him enormously, and also your Mum who often turned up to help out with the merchandise at gigs. Real people in an unreal world.

I really don't have much to criticise or paddle your arse about, other than that you did extremely well to survive your soundbite during the punk period about how you would be 'voting conservative next time' as you defied the conventional punk ethic which inferred everything in the Labour garden to be lovely and everything else a capitalist hell-hole. Love thy Labour was becoming a cliché in pop, and even the integrity of The Clash got tarnished with some of their over-used political ideas.

I inherited you and The Jam in the late seventies for PR. It was a difficult period in your lives, when you were traditionally covered in spit and being voted the angry young man most likely to succeed Townshend. We worked on the *Modern World* album together, which sadly was not one of your best, and sounded as though you had been pressurised into getting something out fast by your record company.

Having represented The Who for over a decade, I suppose it was inevitable I would get the 'young pretenders' even if it was just for a few months. You fell over your own feet a little over Townshend, but then if you were going to have an idol it might just as well have been one of the best.

'I wasn't trying to copy him,' you once told me. 'But I idolised him. I loved the way he moved on-stage and everything The Who did before *Tommy* was something special so it was natural I was influenced.'

Personally I felt it was a great shame you seemed unable to sit it out longer with the other Jam members, Paul Buckler and Bruce Foxton, because you had that unbeatable combination of anger, passion and pain which unified and motivated so many of the great sixties bands and enabled them to mature. The missing ingredient seemed to be humour.

You thrived on acrimony, and are still cutting the mustard as a solo singer-songwriter for the very reason you achieved your initial success with the kids. Your secret formula for success is the same as just about every worthwhile rock and roll composer since the beginning of time — anger plus compassion plus honesty equals empathy.

Be lucky

Keith

EDDY
GRANT

Eddy enjoys a chuckle
with former England cricket
captain Mike Gatting.

EDDY GRANT

GUYANA'S ONE-MAN BAND

Dear Eddy,

For an eight-year-old kid who arrived in Stoke Newington in the fifties with nothing more than a pocket full of buttons which you won as the self-styled 'marble champion of Guyana' to end up in the nineties as one of the richest singer–songwriter–musicians in the world, living in the largest plantation house on Barbados with your own recording studio in which the Stones, Sting and The Thompson Twins record, is 'not too shabby', as they say down Highbury way.

There was one delightful story on your arrival as an eight-year-old from your two-room house in Guyana in the fifties, to your new home in a row of terraced houses in North London. 'Why has our new house got all these doors?' you asked your father with bewilderment surveying the line of joined-together dwellings.

So what were you like to look after during the glory years of 'I Don't Wanna Dance', 'Electric Avenue' and 'Gimme Hope, Jo'anna' when I was your press agent? You were mostly a delight to represent, despite the traditional curse of the singer–songwriter which seems to turn self-belief into blind obstinacy. Self-reliance is your strength, but it's also your Achilles heel (along with some odd superstitions stemming from your dream that it will mean bad luck if you cut your waist-length dreadlocks).

If ever a man went to work under the banner of 'My Way', it was you, from the moment you switched from playing your father's favourite instrument — the trumpet — to carving your own guitar out of a lump of wood at school and attempting to emulate your boyhood hero Chuck Berry. Remember how we ran into 'loveable' old Chuck in the nineties in a London club just after you had written a number called 'Chuck is King' which we got them to play on the house system while he was there? I politely enquired of the hugely talented but sadly paranoid Mr Berry, who was sitting on his own staring into space, if he would care to meet you. 'Boy,' he said, (I was forty-seven at the time) 'Boy — can't you see ahm relaxing?' Sure thing.

Mr Berry then refused to sign a young fan's autograph — 'Cos you're too ugly,' and I retired. Sad such a hero to so many should be so ungracious. Your other great hero, who happens to be one of mine, is Muhammad Ali, whom both of us had the luck to meet. Unfortunately, great talent and great men do to not always go together like Ali. One of Chuck Berry's more quotable lines was that if he had the chance to 'do it all over again', he would take a course in business studies and then learn to play the guitar. It is something which you had to learn the hard way.

A near-death experience has a wonderful way of focusing the mind, and after having written the classic number-one hit, 'Baby Come Back' in 1968 for your group The Equals (two-tone before anyone ever thought of it), and eight more top-thirty hits including 'Viva Bobby Joe' and 'Black Skin Blue Eyed Boys', you had a minor heart attack. You made the mistake of getting back on-stage after a bad car crash too soon, but it made you completely re-think the strains of life. You realised that too much reliance on others caused you further stress and anxiety, so you seized control of as many pieces of your own cake as you could by forming your own record label, Ice Records, plus becoming your own producer, publisher, promoter and manager. You even went to the extent of distributing your cult hits like 'Message Man' off the back of lorries in Guyana, the Caribbean and Africa. In the studio you literally became a one-man band by writing, singing, playing and arranging everything.

When it became obvious that distribution was just more stress, you relinquished that responsibility with reluctance and 'Living on the Front Line' became your first major solo hit. You began to assume the status of role model to other aspiring black artistes in the UK who realised they could crack the system if they had your guts and tenacity. You summed up your philosophy neatly in an *NME* interview with Paul Du Noyer in 1982 when you said: 'Only the people in the streets should be able to write off an artiste. With my music I have always tried to be directly responsible to the people and not the media or the managers or the record company bosses. It may sound presumptuous but if you can get yourself into a position of control and freedom to express yourself it will work for you.'

In the late eighties you were also successful in buying back all the copyrights to your early songs held by the late and highly respected music publisher, Eddy Kassner, so that you now own every song you have ever written. Kassner was no slouch when it came to picking up copyrights, and had bought the rights to a completely unknown song called 'Rock Around the

Clock' in the fifties, but he liked you.

'He was not a man to let go of anything easily,' you told me once, 'But I liked him and I learnt from him and he knew it, which was why he let me buy my music back. Kassner was the old style of Jewish business man in the music business. He was tough but he had heart. He enabled me to do something not even Paul McCartney has been able to achieve — own everything I ever wrote.'

It is not unreasonable that following your early heart scare a man who had previously been a keen footballer (indeed your brothers Rudy and Alpine were pro-standard) and left your mark on many a shin guard (my own included) with your Ice Records team should look for healthier and sunnier climes. You found them in the early eighties in Barbados. What you and your wife Anne, plus your four children, found was the biggest run-down plantation house on Barbados. Called 'Bayleys', the original owner was hanged in 1861 from a huge tree which still dominates the garden by the families of the very slaves he had given the same summary justice. It seemed poetic justice that eventually a black man should own his house. Hopefully the old slave driver is now spinning in his grave.

'Blue Wave Recording Studios', which you built adjacent to your house, is constructed on the site of the old slave quarters where the 'boys' were chained up at night after working in the sugar cane fields. It was here that you recorded, wrote and produced *Killer on the Rampage* and subsequent hits like 'Gimme Hope, Jo'anna', and where the Rolling Stones came to record whilst I was your press agent.

'The Eddy Grant Barbados Junket', as it became known in the press during the eighties, was the last of the great freebie trips when we all had first-class tickets hurled into our laps for overseas tours by record companies deluged by the mighty dollar. You were never a great philanthropist when it came to distributing your own 'dosh' to the media but were happy to be assisted. Careful examination would uncover a great many credits on album sleeves for the likes of Caribbean Airways, and free accommodation could usually be found from a tourist board anxious to promote Barbados. It was always deemed to be 'unfortunate' for journalists I took out that they had to go for a full week, as free package flights were always constructed more cheaply on a weekly return. During some of the 'lulls' in your career it was never hard to get you national press — most of my conversations with them for you went like this:

'How would you like to interview Eddy Grant?'

'Latest single isn't doing much.'

'How would you like to interview Eddy Grant in Barbados?'

'When do we leave, and can I take a photographer?'

You are an astute judge of people but I was extremely wary of one European journalist I had inherited from EMI's overseas department who arrived separately on our first press trip. My first sight of the balding, diminutive figure of 'Bernie' — all four foot nine inches of him, dressed in leather shorts and braces, and smothered from head to foot in rock and roll badges — was as he circled you like a munchkin at disembarkation, gazing upwards and pulling your dreadlocks, muttering, 'I have a dog at home like this!'

I hastily introduced you to a photographer who ingratiated himself by taking shots of you from what he announced was your 'best side', whilst 'Bernie' did another circular tour and announced emphatically: 'He does not have a best side.' You promptly cracked up — thank God for artistes with a sense of humour about themselves. We prematurely assumed on first acquaintance that 'Bernie' was bonkers and dubbed him 'ET' and kept him at a reasonable distance. You, however, were much more perceptive and merely smiled and declared his deadpan humour made you laugh, and we should reserve judgement.

Next morning at the Casuarina Beach Club Hotel my press party were gathered outside under the palm trees sipping breakfast orange juice on a bright sunny day in almost a hundred degrees of heat. Suddenly, 'Bernie' emerged from his room and crossed the lawn towards us dressed in snow boots, full length white skiing outfit, complete with leather helmet and ski goggles. A hotel waiter, trained to be courteously impassive, managed to contain himself until he had passed 'Father Christmas' little helper', and then creased up before dropping his tray and running into the hotel with his hands clamped over his mouth.

Puzzled, one of our party asked Bernie when he reached the breakfast bar why he was wearing the ski goggles. 'To keep the glare off the snow of course,' he explained, as though to a child. Over the next few days we discovered Bernie spoke about four languages fluently, was University educated, and was an experienced photo-journalist who had been all round the world. He was extremely intelligent, kind and generous, and lived with his leopard in Zurich. Yes, a leopard. Gradually we realised he had made a virtue out of his small stature by his eccentric dress and behaviour, so he went from being odd man out to the best-loved person in the party. Any attempt by locals to belittle Bernie who made the same initial mistake that we had was met by a chorus of disapproval and rapid defence. We were rightly ashamed of our first reaction, and you were right, of course.

'You see,' you said, with a knowing smile after I had told you of our rapid reassessment on your tennis court. 'Never judge a book by its cover. What is more, he does have a breed of dog whose fur grows just like my dreadlocks, and he believes both sides of my face are equal — thus, no good side.'

It was at this point Bernie minced up with his camera, proffering a tennis ball as we stood outside the courts by your recording studio. 'Now Eddy,' said Bernie in his heavy Swiss accent, 'I am thinking that it would make a good photo for me if you put this in your mouth.'

'You know what I'm thinking, Bernie?' you grinned.

Stories from those Barbados trips are still legend in the music business, and you contributed your share with your own mischievous sense of humour. I had flown out in 1984 to arrange a press campaign to find the Rolling Stones in residence at your studio. You were aware that I had recently departed from them on none-too-happy terms. I arrived at your house after a six-hour delayed flight, irritable, dripping with perspiration, dressed in a white short-sleeve shirt, baggy khaki shorts, open-toe sandals and wearing a pristine white, panama hat.

'Good to see you, old boy,' you grinned on my shattered appearance in your kitchen. 'I expect you would like to go over to your room and freshen up.' You then explained that my bedroom was across the way above the studios where the Stones were already to be heard in full rehearsal, and the only entrance was through their small rehearsal room.

I was so hot, sweaty, tired and in need of a shower so that it would not have mattered to me if it had been

Margaret Thatcher herself over there, so I just stomped through their rehearsal staring straight ahead until I reached the door at the far end which led to the stairs and my room above. There was a slurring on the keyboards, a discord on guitar and clash of cymbals as they recognised the antiquated colonial apparition before them, and finally Ron Wood broke the stunned silence by exclaiming, 'Fuck me — it's Somerset Maugham.'

Sting recorded his entire *Dream of the Blue Turtles* album at your studio in Barbados and was somewhat mystified by the fact that you called him 'old boy' the whole time; but then you call everyone 'old boy'. He was delighted with the signed framed photograph of you both which he received at the end of the sessions, but was mystified as to why he is out of focus. He maintains to this day that it is very good of you, though.

I can also now reveal to you what the curious greeting was that used to wake you up the early hours of the morning when, across from the studio, through the open bedroom window, ghostly voices would float on the night air calling, 'Good night, Eddy', 'Good night, Eddy', 'Good night, Eddy' for a full ten minutes. It had become a ritual for all Sting's 14 musicians, producers, engineers and recording staff to make an individual salutary abeyance before each of your pictures which grace the exit corridor of the studio before retiring for the night. You thought you were having a recurring nightmare.

Apart from about a dozen trips to Barbados (I managed to convince you that you needed your press agent badly out there) I wound up in some highly unusual places with you due to your multi-national identity which made you an acceptable artiste in territories like Cuba, which we visited in 1985 as guests of Fidel Castro for their annual Music Festival. You were the first major rock artiste to play the country since the coup in 1958. Although it was illegal to take currency out of the country, you were always happy to barter for crystal, wood or tractor parts and ship them back for use on the plantation.

The press trip to Cuba was momentous because it coincided with the most devastating hurricane to hit the island in 25 years. After being rerouted to Newfoundland airport for eight hours while it abated, we arrived in Havana to find no reception committee. I bribed our way on to a coach at the airport and we arrived at our designated hotel to find it had no electricity and our rooms were on the fourteenth floor, without lifts.

It says something for Cuban spirit and English resolve that we managed to co-exist for three days on 'revoltillo' (scrambled eggs to you) as it seemed the only thing the kitchen could whip up without electricity. Cuba was the one communist country out of eight I visited where the people seemed to have no racial hang-ups, and a community spirit which worked. Chaotic damage from that hurricane was cleared up by 'the people' in just a day.

Finally, 'cultural exchange' officials managed to move us to another hotel with power, and as we all marched down the steps to the awaiting coach our hotel lit up like a Christmas tree. All this was made all the more irritating by the fact that you were able to sit out the entire hurricane at home in Barbados which was only two hours flying time away, and simply wait until things cleared up. When you turned up in time for your concert, fresh as a daisy having sat out the hurricane's effects at home, it was to an unshaven, poorly-fed and slightly dejected press party, huddling together in the bar drinking warm beer.

'Been a spot of rain, old boys?' you asked innocently. You were lucky not to get lynched. Needless to say, you were later rapturously acclaimed by ten thousand Cuban youths to the extent that one paper proclaimed it 'the kind of reception normally given to heroes of the revolution'.

Having not heard from you for a year (presumably you were having too good a time), it was coincidental that you should come on the phone just as I was writing this. 'Never far from pain,' of course you were able swiftly to inform me that you had a cold sore on your lip. For the fittest and most healthy man of your age I have met, you are also a terrible hypochondriac. There then followed an hysterical impersonation of Mick Jagger — you do a great Jagger impression, just don't let him ever catch you — whom you took to the test match in Guyana last year. He seemed impressed by the fact that even when doors refused to open for him, he only had to mention your name in the country of your birth to get a front-row ticket.

'You big out here, aintcha?' asked Jagger adenoidley, and you had to admit modestly that you were indeed, 'Big back home, old boy.' At one time you owned the country's only bus service, but I understand you now just own a hotel.

I recall you trying to persuade Mick during the times that they merely mixed or rehearsed at your studio that the Rolling Stones really should come out and do an entire album there, as 'Blue Wave' was now one of the most advanced in the world and certainly in lovelier surrounds than Air London in Montserrat — plus no volcano. You added that of course having the Rolling Stones record an entire album would be a big plus for the studio. Mick's response was, 'I know what you mean, Ed, it would be a real *cachet*.'

You are one artiste I can honestly say I do not begrudge one cent of what you have earned or one iota of your fame. You are a perfect role model for any aspiring young popular musician trying to make it on their own terms, and having done so whilst remaining a decent human being first and a gifted artiste second.

Good health, old boy

Keith

SCOTT
WALKER

SCOTT WALKER

THE GRETA GARBO OF POP

Dear Scott

What a wasted talent you were — the man who should have, could have, but never did and always hid. The Greta Garbo of pop. The Walker Brother who was the most gifted young vocalist of the sixties and might have been the new Sinatra. An early Eddie Fisher protégé in America (until he lost interest when his wife, Elizabeth Taylor ran off with Richard Burton), you were strangely likened to the late Dean Martin.

It is almost incredible now to recall that in the sixties we spoke in the same breath of the Beatles, the Rolling Stones and the Walker Brothers. If you could have only have assumed a disguise like Jagger or McCartney which protected your private life and enabled you to interact with your teenage audience (at one time your fan club numbers in the UK exceeded those of the Beatles), I have no doubt that you could have made the same transition that Sting and Robbie Williams made years later. You unfortunately had no on-stage armour.

You were a baritone who even in the nineties was revered by contemporary artistes like Julian Cope, and in the eighties had an album released with the embarrassing but magnificently pretentious title *The Godlike Genius of Scott Walker.*

If you had only been able to live with your romantic image, and coped with singing love songs for a few more years, you might have been a superstar today. Sadly, your experience as a teenage idol with the Walker Brothers in the sixties, and your own insecurities, virtually tore you apart. When I was your PR in the seventies we even had to fake a car crash for you to get you out of fulfilling a live performance in the Midlands of which you were genuinely terrified. Remember the 'concussion'?

You had already made a half-hearted attempt at suicide at your London flat because of stress, so I devised a scheme to get you off the hook from your show with a 'scam' not even your manager knew about. I had someone drive your car into a tree without you in it, and you promptly hit yourself over the head with a brick and checked into the nearest hospital casualty department *en route* for the projected concert in the Midlands. I then released the story to all the news agencies, and photographs were taken of the crashed car and you with a cut on your forehead looking sorry for yourself which appeared in the national press. You were good at looking sorry for yourself in photographs. The whole charade released you from your contractual appearance, and from the fear of appearing live on-stage, which was as genuine then as that which others suffer over heights or flying in planes. You developed a real phobia about audiences, which for a pop singer was tantamount to a shepherd with agoraphobia.

Occasionally you could be found balancing a consoling blonde on one knee and a beer on the other, looking forlorn in clubs like The Scotch of St James in London, but mostly you stayed home forlorn and pulled the curtains in your Chelsea flat. Ironically, I recall you bought the flat because of its apparently quiet residential nature but then awoke after your second week in residence to a noise that sounded as though you had arrived in the middle of the Balkans conflict. Being an American you had not realised the significance of your proximity to Chelsea Football club, and the fact that you backed on to the ground, or what the eventual start of the season meant in terms of support from tens of thousands of fans. You moved out.

Later you acquired a huge St Bernard dog that lived with you on the fourth floor of another flat in Swiss Cottage. Your totally uncontrolled canine would bounce gleefully out of the front door on escaping and pin visitors to the lift doors whilst taking a layer of skin off their face with its tongue. 'Don't worry,' you would announce apologetically, wrestling him off. 'He is just a pup and wants to play.' Only you would keep a dog the size of a grizzly bear, designed for the Himalayan mountain rescue operations on the fourth floor of a high-rise flat.

Contact with the business world was always painful for you as you became more reclusive and you even had me convinced that your phone had developed a fault where you could not make outgoing calls. However if someone spoke you could sometimes return the call later if you had heard. Wonderful nonsense. How you must have rejoiced at the invention of the answer machine and 'screening' calls and cursed the introduction of the mobile phone.

Your solo hits like 'Jo'anna' and 'Jackie' indicated a penchant for the melancholic, soul-searching lyrics of Jacques Brel and Tim Hardin. Your adoring teenage fans wanted you to be a 'romantic' singer, although there were not too many composers writing great 'torch' songs in the sixties, so as a self-confessed existentialist with more enthusiasm for Jean Paul Sartre than Barbara Cartland, you were a contradiction in terms.

Despite your neurotic tendencies, there was a very endearing quality about you as a person which encouraged those of us who knew you to be protective. You were such an emotional mess most of the time that even the hard-bitten national press came to your aid. On one occasion I remember them ignoring a story about your girlfriend being on shoplifting charges because they felt sorry for you. I can just imagine the tabloids doing it today.

I still shudder at my excruciatingly pretentious sleeve notes I wrote for your third solo album, but your obvious anxiety and vulnerability under pressure reduced more than one journalist to mushy prose in your defence. As Jimi Hendrix once put it so succinctly when he toured with you: 'That Scott Walker, he is so cute I just can't wait for him to fall over and graze his knee so I can kiss it better.' Scuze me while I kiss the knee.

I never discovered the root of your problems, but they seemed to stem from your parents' breakup when you were only a kid, and your close but fractious relationship with your mother whom you revered. You were never emotionally tough enough to withstand the stresses and strains of maintaining the game of being an icon, and at one time even went to the extent of shaving your head in order to destroy your image prior to a major UK tour. The shaved head almost gave your manager Maurice King apoplexy on discovering his 'Prince Charming' had turned into 'Scott Vicious' at the barber's. You just wanted to escape living what you knew was the fiction of the teenage idol. You also became terrified of going on-stage.

The first sighting we had of the American Walker Brothers over here was of you with ex-gravedigger and drummer Gary Leeds and co-vocalist John (Maus) who had all affected shaggy hair styles so that you looked like blonde Beatles. You harmonised like teenage Righteous Brothers on *Ready Steady Go* singing 'Love Her' in 1965. It was, ironically, a song that had been originally intended for the Righteous Brothers, who were not as pretty, and it established a musical formula for further hits in a Phil Spector mode which you overworked.

It was initially just a question of the media working out which brother had the voice, and it proved to be you so young music journalists like myself homed in swiftly on what we recognised was another superstar in the making. You had that mournful, moody appeal which provoked instant screamage adoration, but after more massive hit singles like 'Make It Easy On Yourself', 'My Ship is Coming In' and 'The Sun Ain't Gonna Shine Anymore', your sensitive nature recoiled at the phoniness of it all. You were too early for the times.

You were always late and always charming as I discovered on first interviewing you. You whipped off your trademark shades and announced, with a disarming smile, 'Hey, I'm early for this one right?' to be met by sullen stares from Gary and John who had been there punctually two hours ago.

It emerged that you and 'The Maus', as you called him, had worked in a West Coast band with the unlikely name of The Moongooners and issued a frightful single, 'The Moongoon Stomp', on which you sang and played bass. It sank without a trace in America. You were never a part of the surfing set, but ran with Johnny Rivers who was heavily into the biker scene and for a while you and the gang specialised in toppling outside toilets of the rich and famous down their Hollywood garden hills.

You had been a talented artist, and your mother had been less than delighted when you gave up a promising education and came to England from LA after PJ Proby had literally caught up with you in your Ford Thunderbird to persuade you and 'The Leeds' who had already drummed for him in his backing group that England was the place to be to make a buck in the music business.

The Walker Brothers were born out of a conviction that America had to have a response to the Beatles and the Stones, so for a while it looked like you might be it. Petty squabbles were prefabricated in the Press between you and Jagger over who was the bigger star, but in truth you were never keen on even entering the pop idol stakes. You were not the first teenage idol to discover the truth of Keith Richards' famous maxim in latter years that 'everyone wants to be famous until they are', and you were terrified of audiences who demanded an exhibitionist live performance from a natural introvert and recluse.

You got your first big touring break with the Walker Brothers when the Kinks' drummer Mick Avory took exception to having his drum kit kicked all over the stage by Dave Davies and put six stitches in his head on-stage in Cardiff with a drum pedal. The Walkers replaced the Kinks on their aborted tour but having your hair torn out by the audiences screaming so loud that they could not hear you sing was not the kind of recognition you were looking for.

I have never come across a more confused and miserable pop star than you were by 1966 after the novelty of the first hit singles, when you were headlining incongruously over Jimi Hendrix at Finsbury Park Astoria. I found you in your dressing room, clawing at your face in the mirror complaining you were finished with the Walkers and the whole teenage idol nonsense. 'You've seen and heard Hendrix play Keith,' you said to me. 'The man is a genius and we are topping the bill over him — what a joke. The times are changing and they want talent not just faces. I cannot even face myself in the mirror any more.'

Part of the problem for you was that you had genuine song-writing ability, but little time for commercial compromise. And although you happened to possess one of the great romantic voices of the decade you did not want to exploit it.

Twenty years later I noticed coincidental parallels with another of my clients who had managed to go his own way. Both of you played bass. Both quit an internationally successful trio. Both of you were jazz aficionados. Both of you were literate. Both of you dyed your hair blonde initially. Both of you turned your backs on being a teenage idol.

Both of you were singer–songwriters. Sting, however, was born into the right era, tougher mentally and stayed the course until he was strong enough to break free and seize the iniative for his own ambition.

You, my friend, were never made for those times, but that did not make you a bad person — just over-sensitive and unlucky. The one thing I learnt about you in the early days was that if someone wanted to be your friend, they only had to do one thing. Leave you alone.

Goodbye, and good luck, wherever you are.

PS
You might try asking Sting
to produce your next CD
before it's too late.

Keith

ADAM
FAITH

Keith peruses the paper with
Adam Faith in Tangiers.

ADAM FAITH

LITTLE BIG MAN

Dear Adam,

How are you, mush? How does one sum you up over a relationship which has spanned thirty years? You are little, lethal, and lovable. It was advisable in the early years to look both ways before crossing a road with you, as some of your former squashed friends might testify, for where you led, others got run over.

Charmers often lead a charmed life, and you had your fair share of luck as you were re-plumbed (best advert for a heart bypass I have ever met), resurrected (a near-fatal car crash in the seventies) and reinvented from an early sixties teenage idol with over thirty hit singles to a talented actor with movies like *McVicar* and *Stardust*, musicals like *Alfie* and two enormously successful TV series in *Budgie* and *Love Hurts* in the nineties with Zoe Wanamaker.

I personally thought your re-emergence following your heart bypass to play the all-singing, all-dancing lead in *Alfie* in the eighties was one of the bravest acts I have seen from someone recovering from major surgery a few months previously. You deserved your standing ovation that opening night as much for your courage as your performance.

Later you became financial city columnist for the *Daily Mail* and wrote 'every bloody word, cock', produced albums with Dave Courtney for Roger Daltrey, Lonnie Donegan and Leo and spent your spare time piloting a helicopter ('wound up upside-down in a tree, cock') and scuba-diving ('nearly bloody drowned, mush').

In your time you were a teenage idol with over thirty top-twenty hit singles to your name who subsequently discovered Sandie Shaw (in your dressing room, as I recall), managed Leo Sayer with such a devotion that valuable paintings disappeared off the wall at home, unbeknown to your wife, just to keep him afloat when things got tough. I introduced you to Roger Daltrey early on, who promptly did an entire album of Leo's songs which produced his solo hit, 'One Man Band' written by Leo and recorded at Roger's studio in Burwash.

When things got difficult, I eventually inherited Leo's PR from you. The problem with Leo was that he had a voice like Rod Stewart with the stage persona of Norman Wisdom, and as soon as he dispensed with the clown make-up some of his credibility went with it so that many of the kids began to think of him as a sort of singing Keith Chegwin. Not only did he look like comedian Bobby Ball without the moustache, you could be forgiven for thinking he seemed to want to be him.

Dispensing good advice without due consideration is another characteristic which can lead to repercussions as when Sir Paul McCartney brought Michael Jackson to your home as a guest and you promptly advised 'Whacko' to invest in publishing. He swiftly left, and even more swiftly bought all the Paul McCartney and John Lennon songs he could get his hands on. Sound advice, mind you, and Sir Paul had after all acquired all of Buddy Holly's publishing.

In the fifties the English pop star was a pale imitation of Elvis, and we were cursed with the likes of Marty, Cliff, and Billy Fury all doing weak imitations. What we wanted was someone who came on at least looking like a man, and you suddenly appeared on a black-and-white TV show called *Drum Beat* looking a rock and roll James Dean. We all wanted to be James Dean.

You looked like one of the lads and you had the nerve to nick Cliff Richard's girlfriend, Jackie, and marry her. One of your best moves.

Years later I discovered that you fought like fury to gain yourself some cred with 'the boys' rather than just being another screamage idol. Unfortunately, your manager Eve Taylor, who made Margaret Thatcher look like Mary Poppins, believed in the established teenage pop formula and you fought a losing battle with a woman who both bolstered and undermined you for many years.

Your desire to be accepted as a more macho pop star, and your early interview with John Freeman on his infamous *Face to Face* TV slot, gave you unusual gravitas and respect in the sixties as the first thinking pop star. You broke the traditional mould of the singing simpleton established by Peter Sellers on his comedy LP playing 'Twit Conway' as the idiot pop star. You transparently had some ideas of your own and could express them.

Our friendship was established in the early sixties when the teen magazine *Fabulous*, for which I was writing, hit on the staff-friendly formula of sending pop stars on short holiday breaks and writing up the results. We travelled to Tangier with your agent Maurice Press and photographer Bill Francis. We all still reminisce about that trip some thirty years later, like veterans of some foreign campaign, because they were some of the funniest days of our lives. It is almost impossible to convey to others the empathy which the four of us enjoyed on that trip or the juvenile but harmless humour. We still fall on the floor at the mention of innocuous phrases and recall the stories of the camel rides, the belly dancers and the snake with the kind of nostalgia that is born of youthful indiscretion and boys behaving badly.

Humour and charm are your two most potent assets, and I have literally seen you charm birds out of trees. Women are absolute suckers for your charisma and fall adoringly at your feet when you turn on the smile. Any man who ever suffered from a sense of low self esteem because of being short should have taken a workshop in how to inch ahead from you.

Living as I did in a thoroughly conventional suburb of Ewell my neighbours were often confused and a little bewildered by the appearance of well-known faces pulling up outside the house. 'Excuse me, but why was Adam Faith standing in my front garden piddling on my rose bush yesterday afternoon?' enquired an intrigued but perplexed next door neighbour one morning.

'Ah yes,' I explain. 'Well, you see, he wanted me to carry on listening to his solo CD in his Rolls and would not let me out to let him into my house, and he got caught short and he is rather impetuous ...'

'Quite,' she replies 'Well if he gets a thorn in it, no doubt it will help him into character for his next series of *Love Hurts*.'

Your arrival that morning began with an insane conversation which I recorded on my answer phone, and is a good example of your *ad hoc* sense of humour. I had originally arranged to see you at your family home in Sussex, and we were going for a 'lovely lunch in a little French restaurant I know, and then come back to the house and do the interview, mush.' I was not hugely surprised to get a frantic phone call on my answering machine the night before our arrangement telling me that plans had changed and you would do the chat in your car and you would pick me up from my home.

The phone rings and it is you wanting directions: 'Right, I am going under a bridge now so give me directions from there ...'

'Don't go through the traffic lights, turn right ...'

'I'm going through the lights now ...'

'I said don't go through the lights, do a right ...'

'Is there a purple car on my right-hand side?

'How the hell would I know in my hall from a mile away?'

'Don't get nasty, mush. I've turned right. Is there a milk float coming out of the road? You go out in the middle of the road and wave to me.'

Further absurd directions are requested which drive me apoplectic as you claim to be going the wrong way down another motorway, when I suddenly notice through my hall window your cumbersome great Rolls is trying to squeeze into my tiny driveway, while you are still asking for directions on your mobile whilst regaling me about speeding juggernauts, which are supposedly passing you on the M25.

Briefly I showed you some clippings and photographs from our scuffling days in Tangier during the sixties, and other chance meetings which you had forgotten when we were both in our late teens at events you played like 'The Great Pop Prom' which used to take place at the Albert Hall every year. There I am backstage with quiffed hair, with you dressed in a casual jacket and polo shirt as I shepherd you through a group of fans clamouring for autographs.

'Strewth,' you commented. 'You kept all this lot — that's great. Should make a great book.' Funny you should mention that, Terry.

'Must have it.'

Keith

PHIL
COLLINS

Phil Collins
with *Genesis*.

PHIL COLLINS

SUPER-BLOKE

Dear Phil,

'Wot a nice bloke!' You must cringe every time you hear
or read it now, but if it is the worst thing they can say
about you after thirty years in the music business it
can't be too bad. I am deeply suspicious of superstars
with a 'nice' image, but yours seems the real thing, or
you should be up for an Oscar.

The rock star with 'the common touch'. God, how
it must get up your nose. I liked your riposte to one
journalist asking if you could really be as nice as most
people painted you. 'Why don't you ask my ex- wife,'
you responded, having been recently divorced.

Although you dropped early aspirations as a child
actor playing the Artful Dodger in a West End
production of *Oliver* (must be something about that role,
the late Anthony Newley, the late Steve Marriot (Small
Faces), Davey Jones (The Monkies), and Robbie
Williams being other Dodgers), something of the 'likely
lad' and the 'cheeky chappie' stuck.

You were marooned like a penguin in the midst of
a public school desert when you joined Genesis in 1971

when it was formed by ex-students of the exclusive English public school Charterhouse (old boys included the composer Vaughan Williams and the late England Cricket captain Peter May). You were of the opinion you had been brought in for 'light relief'. For a few brief months, courtesy of your late lovable record company boss Tony Stratton Smith, I was your PR for the semi-pretentious nonsense that became the *Nursery Cryme* album. Although I liked Messrs Bank, Rutherford and Gabriel for their articulate nature and their cultured manners (you should at least finish Charterhouse with those), a band writing songs about 'The Return of the Giant Hogweed' with a lead singer with a shaven forehead and a penchant for dressing up on stage as giant petunia was strange company.

You came into your own when Peter Gabriel went to do his own thing and you suggested that you might be able to handle the vocals whilst keeping your drum hand in with your splinter group Brand X and guesting with the likes of Eno, John Cale, Howard Jones, Adam Ant and Eric Clapton to name but a few. You ate up the session work and discovered that in addition to your percussive skills you had the most important ingredients of all when it came to pop success — charisma, a distinctive voice and commercial nonce.

A little melancholic self-martyrdom goes a long way for a singer in popular music, as Frank Sinatra and Scott Walker can testify, but you managed to hit the bullseye by homing in on the touchy and untried territory of divorce with your two solo albums *Face Value* and *Hello I Must Be Going*. For writers with your kind of veracity, personal experience is the key to the kind of anger and compassion you injected into this thorny subject, which rang bells with those of us who have been through that particular hell with children caught in your wake. You were something of a sounding board for the 'torn apart', and your little anthems of self-pity touched anyone who had been through a painful break-up.

For a few years we would bump into each other backstage with Sting and the Stones, where you were widely welcomed by other artistes as a friendly face and I would generally detect your presence when I got lifted into mid-air from behind, by the elbows (drummers have very strong forearms) with a cry of, 'Oi, Keith, how's it going?' — a painful but friendly method of greeting.

There was one occasion when I worked above your agency 'Solo' in Fulham and had been downstairs to see if I could purchase a pair of good tickets for one of your forthcoming London concerts at the Palladium only to discover they had sold everything. However I was assured that if there were any returns they would let me know immediately. Meanwhile, I hit on a little ruse of sending to your home a photograph of the cast of *Tommy* which I had publicised, in which you had played Uncle Ernie in striped blazer with blacked-out teeth, and were depicted with other stars like Elton John, Stevie Winwood, Roger Daltrey, John Entwistle, Pattie Boulaye, Pete Townshend and Billy Idol. I included a grovelling note of apology for the delay and a PS to the effect I had been trying to buy a couple of tickets for your concert without success and wondered if 'you had any influence'.

The weeks went by with no reply, and tickets became available through the agency which I bought and thought no more of the matter as I had plenty of other things on my plate.

The tabloids were having a field day with a rather embarrassing situation Eddy Grant had got himself into, and I could not get out the door of my house and into the office for fending them off one morning. Finally I reached the other side of my front door only to hear the bloody phone ring again, and I dashed back inside to field another press enquiry.

'Yes,' I yelled in exasperation.

'Sorry to ring you at home,' the call began in the familiar journalist formula, 'It's Phil.'

'Phil who?' I bellowed deafeningly down the phone.

'Er, Phil Collins. I've got a couple of tickets for you and wondered whether you would like to be my guest tomorrow night at my show?' That what you get for being a 'nice bloke'.

Now it appears you have left these shores for Geneva, complete with stocks of marmite and HP sauce, to save your family from further intrusive journalists anxious to turn 'Mr Nice' into 'Mr Nasty'. The crunch came when the hard news boys camped in the garden of your new girlfriend's house whilst her father and grandfather were dying of cancer, and staked out your ex-wife and daughter so that she was unable to get out of her front door and go to school. It was a time your good humour finally deserted you.

Au revoir

Keith

BILLY
IDOL

BILLY IDOL

SUPER-LIP

Dear Billy,

Sometimes I can spot an unstoppable face in this business instantly, and you had that thick-lipped, slack-jawed, high-cheekboned, blonde sex-appeal that was a perfect fit for the punk idol identikit in the seventies. 'The Blond Bombshell', as you became known, could switch hair dye from red to yellow to black and back, but eventually settled on an image which was caught midway between a recruit for the Hitler Youth and Cliff Richard's unacceptable kid brother.

Unfortunately, even by Johnny Rotten's standards, you possessed the most tuneless voice I have ever heard on stage. You did have that look, though, and your group Generation X managed to play at such a volume that your flat vocals were drowned in the din. You projected like a young Elvis with built-in sneer but were in fact introvert and shy so that it was unsurprising to learn that your previous claim to musical fame was as a member of your school's folk club in Worthing where your big number was 'The Frog He Would A-Courting Go'.

Ten years later you emerged from an 'image lift' in

Los Angeles as the teenage sex-god in black leather, chains and pelvic thrusts as the boy with the 'whiplash smile', and lo someone had taught you almost to sing in tune. The result was *Rebel Yell* which portrayed you as sort of young biking Brando, all mean machine and no brakes. The Hollywood dream machine had given you an image that you actually seemed to believe in, and you obligingly posed on huge motorbikes and promptly fell off them breaking your leg. Good try, though.

The 'black sheep boy' your management invented for you had even assumed a West Coast American accent and attitude to match when I met you backstage at the Albert Hall where you were playing Cousin Kevin in The Who's rock opera some years later. You were both funny and frightening — the image had apparently taken over the man, or at least it was a convincing performance of braggadocio.

The *News of the World* now regularly trots out lines like MP'S GIRL IN SEX ROMP WITH IDOL, and your predictably tawdry image sails on. Shame, I liked you as William Broad, but then I suppose there is not much of a market for shy lads singing 'The Frog He Would A-Courting Go'. Be careful you do not let them turn you into a joke, or is it already too late?

Rock and roll, man ...

Keith

DUANE
EDDY

DUANE EDDY

BIG TWANGER

Dear Duane,

My very first interview as a nineteen-year-old reporter for IPC teen magazines in 1960 was a 'double header' with you as the bestselling instrumental rock guitarist in the world, and the man being tipped as the new young Frank Sinatra — the late Bobby Darin, who had just been voted best newcomer of the year for his hit, 'Mack The Knife' in a musical poll.

You, however, were my first real teenage electric guitar hero (saving Bert Weedon's memory) from my Brylcream days when I thrust threepenny bits (five plays for a shilling) into the only jukebox in Tolworth at the Blue Star Café, and your instrumental bass guitar riffs bulged the Wurlitzer's canvas-covered speaker. You sold millions of instrumentals like 'Rebel Rouser', 'Forty Miles of Bad Road' and 'Peter Gunn Theme'. The twang was the thang in the late fifties in my school yard.

Whilst on the staff of *NME* in the sixties, we had one journalist who specialised in grabbing the albums. He knew little about who the artiste was, and specialised in minimalistic reviews from the sleeve notes rather than play the records. There was a classic 'clanger' when he reviewed one of your instrumental compilations with the one-liner, 'Duane has never been in better voice than on this collection.'

London Records decided to throw a joint press reception at the Savoy for their two biggest visiting American artistes, and whilst I was unmoved by 'Mr Ring a Ding Ding Jr' and his middle-aged hep-cat antics, I was thrilled about the chance to interview you. You were the first to be thrown to the press for a chat, and we were afforded a brief 15 minutes each to obtain quotes. I discovered to my frustration that, though unfailingly polite, you were painfully shy and monosyllabic to the extent that most questions were answered 'Yep' or 'Nope'.

Extracting a quote was like trying to draw teeth, and I was seriously considering quitting music journalism then and there. Suddenly 'mouth almighty' Darin swept into the reception to make his contribution and produced instant copy: 'I shall be a legend by twenty-five and dead by thirty' (he made thirty-seven); 'I am expecting to win an Oscar next year', 'I don't like these comparisons with Sinatra. I am a better actor, a better singer and a better dancer, what is more I am better looking ...' At least I had a feature, even if it was not my teenage hero.

Twenty-six years later I was representing an anonymous but highly talented trio of sound engineers, musicians and producers who worked under the collective title of 'Art of Noise' (Anne Dudley, Gary Langan and JJ Jeczalik) who had a top-ten hit with 'Close to the Edit' and another with Prince's composition 'Kiss' featuring Tom Jones. At this time they were reworking your hit 'Peter Gunn Theme', so the man who was almost my journalistic nemesis was flown over for me to arrange interviews with to publicise this cover version. I shook in unhappy anticipation of the return of Duane 'Yep' Eddy twenty years later.

It was with some trepidation that I turned up for our rematch at a London hotel in the nineties and discovered you were as unfailingly polite as ever but had grown a beard, put on some weight and to my enormous relief had learnt to talk, so that the quotes now flowed like wine.

'Guess I must have sold over sixty million records worldwide now, but I signed away all the royalties of my early hits without realising what I was doing ... I used to know Elvis in the days when they called his records "race music", remember talking to him about stereo and he hated stereo. He said mono was boss because it put everything out front musically ... we couldn't afford an echo chamber on my early hits like "Movin and Groovin" and "Cannonball", so I used to climb in this big old rusty water tank in the studio and play inside it.'

John Entwistle of The Who used to say you were his first and last guitar hero.

Twangs for the memory

Keith

DONOVAN

DONOVAN

BOB'S YOUR UNCLE

Dear Don,

You were teleported to instant fame on the TV show
Ready Steady Go in 1965 after being discovered by Geoff
Stephens and Peter Eden 'beatnicking' around St Ives in
Cornwall. When I completed my first interview with
you in a pub off Denmark Street you were carrying your
battered Gibson guitar embossed with 'This Machine
Kills' and wearing a denim cap which gave further fuel
to the 'Kid Dylan' press slur.

For a time there in the sixties as a 'journo' you
almost had me, and a few million others, seduced by
the soppy superficial hippie notion of flower power and
the idea that peace and love might actually make people
think twice about making war and trying love. Like
trying to 'Catch The Wind' really, wasn't it?

There was however, something innocent and childlike about your style as a teenager, and together with
your friend 'Gipsy' Dave you made a John Steinbeck
coupling just short of *Of Mice and Men*. 'Gipsy' had hit
the road with you from Hertfordshire and thence to the
South Coast where you were eventually overcome by
Bob Dylan and his protest creed.

Comparisons with you and Dylan were quite cruel and callous in a press who knew that as an eighteen year old you had neither his experience, political insight or scathing social comment. In fact it was your childlike appeal, looks and approach which were responsible for your initial success, plus record producer Mickie Most's uncanny ability to develop a catchy riff and market the right artiste at the right time.

Mickie Most was the record producer with the golden ear for a commercial single during the sixties, and with both hands on the financial tiller sailed you into the teenage sunset with million-selling singles like 'Colours', 'Sunshine Superman', 'Jennifer Juniper', 'Hurdy Gurdy Man' and 'Sunny Googe Street' which established you as a curly-haired pop idol. You rode out the copy-cat Dylan taunts with albums like *From a Flower to a Garden* (I still have my autographed copy from 'Donovan the folk singer to Keith the Penpusher) and *HMS Donovan* which at least had you taken seriously by the hippie counter-culture in America who on the release of 'Mellow Yellow', began smoking banana peel in misguided empathy. It was also after one of your concerts in America when the kids threw flowers at you that a critic coined the phrase 'flower power'. You were of those times, and stuck with them.

It was evident when I used to interview you at your home on Wimbledon Common that you were donning the mantel of a prophet for the peace and love generation. 'Gipsy' who brewed the tea and made the toast was along for the ride but not fooled by the beautiful people in the record business. 'These people are spending Don's money like water and just agree with anything he says,' he muttered conspiratorially to me once over his beans. 'They are robbing him — no one tells him the truth any more.'

You became huge in the States and your 'Love Ins' at the Carnegie Hall and Madison Square Gardens where you appeared in kaftan and beads established you further as the young Messiah of the flower power cult. Not always saint-like, though. I remember you trying to cure the loveable little Lulu of her virginity in a recording studio, you only received a shriek and a slap. She remained an endangered species in the sixties.

Once the 'giggling guru' had been unearthed by the Beatles and the Beach Boys and turned into a pop star saviour, off you 'Beatled' with the rest of the impressionables like Mia Farrow, Mike Love, John Lennon and Paul McCartney to the ashram in India where the Maharishi Mahesh Yogi eventually blotted his copy book by allegedly jumping on a female celebrity — all in the best possible taste, of course, and for her own spiritual well-being I feel sure. Ringo, who had the only atom of common sense amongst the love-bombed, was the first to bale out and declare the Maharishi's meditation centre was more 'like Butlins', and you returned with the message that it was the system not the man which mattered. You eventually sacked Gipsy who was one of the few honest voices around after a dispute which caused the normally placid minder to drive his Range Rover into your brand new Mercedes on exit. He came and lived in my drive in his converted post office van for a few weeks, but that's another story.

Your heavy-petal double album *From a Flower to a Garden* was redeemed by the inclusion of some traditional nursery rhymes and songs for children like 'Winking Blinking and Nod' and 'The Owl and the Pussycat' which are just as appealing to children today. You would make a wonderful children's presenter and entertainer for some enterprising TV channel.

After the dizzy heights of huge open-air music festivals and the rather grandiose productions in the Albert Hall, Madison Square Gardens and Carnegie Hall, you lost touch, although comebacks have abounded. I inherited you briefly for a few months when the late Jo Lustig tried to relaunch you in the early eighties on a series of one-man shows starting in Windsor but you never really took off again. You became more practical and in touch with your real tough little Glaswegian self. The boy who had fought polio as a kid and won.

Living in America for some years, you pragmatically decided to educate your daughters in England and so had returned with your wife Linda and her son Julian (fathered by the late Rolling Stone, Brian Jones) and two beautiful daughters Astrella and Oriole.

However impractical and pretentious the message of love and peace in the sixties, your message was a great deal more palatable than that being spat out now by some of the gangsta rap, techno and jungle janglers in the US who have replaced it largely with hate and violence, which only brutalises the artiste and the listener. You once had the key to something refreshingly innocent. Go find it again because we need a musical shaman to dig up the lost dreams and hopes for this generation. Maybe it is time to return with some songs of brotherly love and hope and to hell with Marilyn Manson and their ilk who only seem to inspire killers with guns.

Peace and love

Keith

JUSTIN HAYWARD

Keith spaced out with
The Moody Blues.

JUSTIN HAYWARD

JUST IN TIME FOR THE MOODY BLUES

Dear Justin,

Well, how are the Glenn Millers of rock and roll and the two white-bearded wonders on flute and drums? I trust you are still happily ensconced in Tommy Steele's old house in Twickenham with dummy copies of *Tommy The Toreador* visible in the bookcase, and the water feature softly pattering away in the courtyard.

You were always a softly-spoken, gentle soul, devoted to your daughter Doremi and wife Marie. You also had a spine of sheer steel when it came to self-preservation, which was essential in the stormy waters of the Moody Blues.

You played as backing guitarist for Marty Wilde's Wilde Cats as a lanky teenager from Swindon and virtually saved the Moody Blues from extinction in the late sixties by writing the classic rock anthem 'Nights in White Satin' on the *Days of Future Passed* album. It started a giant cult following for the group in America, where one crazed fan staked out the venue since the 'Moodies' last tour with countdown placards, announcing the end of the world for your next appearance. You came — Armageddon passed — and he got arrested.

It is an interesting footnote that you did a publishing deal in the early sixties with Lonnie Donegan, during the period you were broke in the summer season working in Marty Wilde's backing group, which saved you from bankruptcy. A year later you had written the classic 'Nights in White Satin' and contributed substantially to a multi-million selling album. You were reaping massive royalties, of which Donegan had a huge chunk. To your credit you never moaned about the lost royalties. You recalled that without Donegan's fifty pound advance at the time, you would have had to pawn your guitar and retire from the music business so you might never have joined the Moody Blues or written those other huge hits. It is amazing how short some other artistes memories are about those who gave them a helping hand when they needed it most. You were not among them.

Aided and abetted by your brilliant producer Tony Clarke you wallowed in a musical sea of psychedelia and spiritual aspirations in the seventies although Ray Thomas' 'boots and braces' outlook stopped things spiralling into outer space. Other members, like mellotronist Mike Pinder, were of a more spiritual bent and fuelled some of the loftier concepts which followed like *In Search of the Lost Chord*, *On The Threshold of a Dream* and *A Question of Balance*.

There is a fascinating book on the Moody Blues for someone who can unite the conflicting factions in the group. I know my friend the late Ray Coleman was intent on producing another arrow to his prolific list of excellent musical biographies by writing it until he came across the musical fault line which runs through the band. The 'old boys' faction (Ray Thomas and

Graeme Edge) who jokingly used to refer to you and John as 'The Hairdressers' were not keen on collaborating. They tend to see their contribution to the group as fundamental and exclusive.

Your early musical identity was established by the use of the hugely unreliable and unique sound of Pinder's mellotron which gave a strange unearthly, wheezing, church-like base for the soaring choral harmonies. There was a lot of spiritual soul-searching going on in the band which could produce a Buddhist one week and a flat earthist the next, although you and John established a strong orthodox Christian base to the band. Pinder eventually quit to find a 'peace of his mind' in California (misdirected) and left his keyboard seat to the brilliant but eccentric inspiration of Swiss synthesizer-player Patrick Moraz. He was a multi-linguist who mixed up his metaphors so that he might ask at breakfast, 'How did you spoke last night?' To which the correct response was: 'Thank you, Patrick, I spoke like a log.'

Prior to your arrival in the Moody Blues when the late Denny Laine vocalised on their number-one hit 'Go Now', the band had reputations as sixties hell-raisers that were second to none, and an invitation to your parties in Wandsworth meant bacchanalia on a grand scale and boys behaving extremely badly. I recall one I attended as a journalist where I visited the bathroom in the dark without electricity in the house and as I turned to feel my way to the toilet I touched a human leg apparently attached to an unconscious, naked young lady who had been wedged securely into the wash basin by her bottom. I mentioned this to your drummer Graeme Edge who, at the time, was preoccupied with shooting arrows from a long bow from another window at some visiting policeman who had been called out over the late-night disturbance. 'All right? Of course she's all right,' said Graeme. 'She loves it there — says there are good vibes in the bathroom — damn — you made me shoot and miss the copper.'

My working relationship with Ray was fractious as he could be funny and friendly with a few drinks in him and obnoxious and threatening with a few more. During a bad day he would become physically intimidating, as he did at our last encounter. He concluded, after due libation, he had received insufficient media attention for himself at one of your Wembley concerts, clamped me in a neck lock, and dragged back to his dressing room for interrogation. The fact that no one wanted to interview him did not seem acceptable. Pathetically funny now, it was extremely frightening at the time.

I informed you that there was no way I could represent the band while Ray continued to be 'unwell', and that was the end of an eight-year association. I liked the Moody Blues, despite their early pretentiousness, and always felt they were underrated in the UK. You all had heart, even Ray, except when his head came unscrewed. I can think of no other band who can claim to have had a re-released album at number one with *Days of Future Past*, and their new album, *Seventh Sojourn* at number two in the US simultaneously. But it was mostly your talent and spine which glued the Moody Blues together.

'Letters I've written, always meaning to send.'

Keith

SPANDAU
BALLET

Keith with Tony Hadley of *Spandau Ballet* **fame.**

SPANDAU BALLET

OLD ROMANTICS, NEW ROLES

Dear Spandau Ballet,

My first thoughts on taking you on were that you might turn out to be a worse bunch of posers than Duran Duran, but there was genuine musical talent in your band and you put on a good show for the punters on stage. You were a joy to look after — keen on football (even got into the *Roy of the Rovers* comic) — and were genuine mates with a good sense of humour.

Gary and Martin were heading for an acting career, but when the music bug bit you formed Spandau with Tony Hadley (vocals), John Keeble (drums), Steve Norman (bass), Gary (guitar) and Martin (bass). For the 'New Romantics' in the eighties, glamour and fashion were all-important, and you had the look and hitched yourself to the latest fad.

You seemed to be genuinely close friends whom I warmed to enormously, particularly on the tour of Australia when I accompanied you with photographer Alan Ballard. There was no doubt that Gary was the musical driving force, but you all contributed, on-stage and off. You also had a fair and decent manager in Steve Dagger who was throwback to the sixties, when the manager was often so close they became like an extra member. We fell out when he thought someone was loading the group expenses from my office, and although I denied it, I later found him to be correct and that I was also being embezzled in the process.

When your group fell out of fashion, as fashionable groups often do, both Gary and Martin returned to acting and scored a success in their roles as the Krays in the movie about the two twin criminals, and Gary made a convincing job of 'the press agent' with Whitney Houston and Kevin Costner in *The Bodyguard*. He admitted later he had based his character on someone we both knew quite well, I was pleased it was not me. Martin is now a TV superstar in *EastEnders*. Strange that he often seems to be cast as tough, when in reality he is a likeable softie.

Drummer John Keeble has incidentally become a talented wicket keeper for 'The Burnbries' charity cricket team, although prone to smashing things if given out by a dubious umpiring decision. Recently Tony, John and Steve entered a legal dispute with Gary over composing rights and royalties, which led to a landmark decision in the High Court in his favour as the principal songwriter. However, I wonder how many times a suggestion or a small contribution is accepted without acknowledgement in the recording studio by 'principal' songwriters? Anyone who has been in the studio with a group would know that this is often how hits come about, and an inspired idea from another source, be it record producer or sideman can turn an average album track into a massive hit single. Songwriters sadly have selective memories on these matters, and a group collaboration is only a group composition when it is credited as such on the label. The bottom line for all contributors is that if you expect a royalty then make sure you have it in writing because verbal understandings are only as strong as the goodwill that exists during the group's lifetime.

Royalty cheques often separate the men from the boys and break up friendships and groups.

'Truly'

Veith

TERENCE TRENT D'ARBY

Terence with Keith's daughter, Nancy.

TERENCE TRENT D'ARBY

THE SILLY TWISTED BOY

Dear Terence,

'Silly twisted boy' was the catchprhase used by one of Peter Seller's characters in the fifties cult radio programme *The Goon Show* which somehow puts me in mind of you during our brief time together in the late eighties. I cannot think of any potential superstar who has managed to snatch failure from the jaws of success like yourself. When I got your press you were crazed as a loon and into any temptation offered to a rising young pop star, at the same time divesting yourself of advisers, managers and anyone capable of controlling an ego the size of your native New York.

You looked the biz, sang like the biz, and even wrote songs like the biz — nothing could stop you but you and you managed that too. You had been voted 'Best Newcomer' of the previous year with a brilliant debut album titled *The Hardline According To ...* which sold 7 million copies worldwide and produced three massive hit singles in 'Wishing Well', 'Dance Little Sister' and 'Sign Your Name'. The follow-up was the monumental turkey so aptly titled *Neither Fish or Flesh*, for which you ingested as much chemical inspiration as possible and produced an indulgence which even Prince and Michael Jackson would have been hard-pressed to exceed. You clung to the silver-topped walking stick which Prince gave you as though it were a magic wand to get you out of trouble.

I was brought in by CBS Records at this point as though I were some sort of PR Red Adair who could put out a fire that was already blazing out of control. The record company was already spooked by your studio extravagances, but incorrectly assumed that with so much going for you they could give you artistic licence and let you loose in Ireland with virtually an open cheque book for your second album. When they heard the results they panicked and tried to re-mix and edit some of the results, vainly searching for a comprehensible hit single.

Neither Fish or Flesh was a masterpiece of pomposity and over-indulgence, and the press was prised to pounce and roast the bighead who had already declared himself a genius. Self-praise is OK when you are ahead of the pack, but Lord help the over-confident creature who falters, because the media smell a wounded artiste from a great distance, and at this stage you were over-exposed, over-hyped and over here.

Your previous manager had given up after being phoned by you late one night in her room in a Paris hotel where you were both guests and requested to purchase condoms for the young lady you had in your room. You were apparently too embarrassed to fend for yourself. Your lady manager, more embarrassed, phoned down to the refined concierge in your five-star hotel who brought up a tastefully arranged number of packets on a silver tray and asked if madam would care to make a selection.

Despite the mess you had got yourself in you were a likeable victim, and your obsession with sixties music and stars like Hendrix, the Stones and The Who was music to this old press agent's ears. You were intelligent, sensitive and, I think, secretly knew that you had blown it. You had a courage born of despair and bravely attempted to bluff it out with an album you knew was doomed. You correctly assumed any attempt at humility now would be sensed as weakness anyway, and you were past the point of no return. You went into your interviews like a man carrying nails to his own crucifixion. You even posed for a picture as though hung on a cross, and caused inevitable offence. You had your heart on your sleeve but both feet still firmly in your mouth. You were in some ways the most quotable artiste I have represented, but you were a real danger to yourself, e.g.:

'So tell me, is it possible to be Prince and not have an ego like that?

'You cannot go on stage and be that dynamic or that powerful without it. I have experienced it and it is almost like possession. You can't help yourself. Good God, Jesus himself might have been an asshole.' Not even John Lennon could have cause more affront with that one. You got sillier.

'Dolphins fuck because they enjoy it — they are smarter than we are.'

'Religion has done more harm than good — I have no time for it.'

'Since the sixties most artistes have turned into businessmen. Dire Straits are as much a brand name as Boots the Chemist.'

'Being a father puts you close to the pulse of life — but I could not bring myself to change Seraphina's nappy.'

'You cannot say acid is as destructive as crack cocaine.'

Tell that to Brian Wilson.

I had an impossible task of redirecting or controlling you at this stage of your career, but I tried because you seemed to me to be more sinned against than sinning, and that was what I was being paid for anyway. You swiftly went to ground in LA before re-emerging a few years later with a couple more hits, but 'there is a time and tide in the affairs of men which taken at the ebb leads on to success', and you missed the boat.

You were never as gifted as you professed, but stronger management might have helped earlier. Now we hear you're to be the replacement for the late Michael Hutchence in the Australian supergroup INXS which has to be the most bizarre substitution I can recall in pop music. You are one of the most singular talents I have encountered and the thought of you being contained within a group is incomprehensible. I predict you will drive each other potty within a year.

Good luck, cobber

Keith

LONNIE
DONEGAN

LONNIE DONEGAN

THE DIY MUSIC MAN COMETH

Dear Lonnie,

I trust the old ticker is still merrily tocking along after all your bypass problems, and you are dreaming up some way of making a comeback so that I can dust off my acoustic guitar and rehash my own versions of 'Rock Island Line' and 'Alabama Bound' which were nicked straight off your records for my group The Rebels at school. It is my considered opinion that you should be carried around in a sedan chair for the rest of your life by other musicians who listened to your advice to 'do it themselves' in a skiffle group. Amongst the talented, stuttering, acne-ridden youths of yesteryear who owe you a life-long debt are Adam Faith, Pete Townshend, Jeff Beck, Elton John, Keith Richards and just about every sixties group guitarist that had a hit. I can even recall an embryonic Jimmy Page aged about 12 playing in a skiffle group at the Co-Op Hall in Tolworth where I lived.

You were indirectly responsible for my ever getting in the music business, because the first album I ever bought was your 'ten incher' on the Pye Nixa label in its hideous green sleeve, and you were the first artiste I ever paid to see for seven shillings and sixpence at the Albert Hall at 'The Great Skiffle Concert' which you headlined with others like The Vipers, Nancy Whisky and Bob Court. You led me and millions of kids to folk and blues artistes like Woodie Guthrie, Sonny Terry and Brownie McGhee and the great Leadbelly, for which much thanks.

I finally met you thirty years later in London when you were 'sampled' by one of Jive Bunny's compilations I worked on, and we had lunch and organised a couple of photo calls. You were a prickly but conversational man with a new baby who believed you failed to get your just deserts from The Chris Barber Band for 'Rock Island Line' ('all I got was a session fee') which put them in the top ten both sides of the Atlantic and fired your solo career.

You, mistakenly in my opinion, went the route of the 'all-round entertainer' too soon after skiffle faltered and lost your folk and blues roots which, together with an original style, gave you musical credibility. That was the way it was then for the ephemeral pop artiste who sought longevity. You were too original an artiste to be turned into a comic song and dance man, though, and 'My Old Man's A Dustman', although the first ever single to go straight to number one in the British charts, was a turn too soon for such an original artiste.

Just a few years ago I saw your one-man show at Bourne Hall in my village of Ewell and enjoyed it immensely, especially the first half devoted to stories and early folk and blues influences in your RAF days. On the day I bought my ticket on the door from a nice bright young teenager and informed him that I had first seen you perform at about his age. 'That's my Dad,' he said proudly, and he had a right to be.

May your chewing gum never lose its flavour,

Keith

PAUL
YOUNG

PAUL YOUNG

IN SEARCH OF THE LOST
VOCAL CHORD

Dear Paul,

Where the hell are you, and what happened to your voice?
I saw you on TV the other night, emaciated, with a scrubby
beard and looking as though you had just got out of
Kosovo — must have been a bad night.

Now, you had a voice that was equally as good as Rod
Stewart's, and you were prettier, a good performer on
stage, and far too talented to be sidelined. I got you very
early on in your career when you were with Streetband
who had a ridiculous hit single called 'Toast', and
consequently spent all my time telling journalists to ignore
the hit and come and listen to the lead singer who had star
written all over him. I hope the rumours about your throat
problems are not correct and your voice has not suffered,
because for such a good voice to disappear would be
tragic.

Later you formed Q Tips and were on a tour I
promoted for The Who when I did a similar but unpaid
number for you by telling journos to arrive early and catch
the singer with the support band. Later I worked in an
office where you were in and out all the time. Always

charming, always polite, always friendly. You were one of
the good guys and should come back.

Go suck a zube, or something

Keith

REG
PRESLEY

REG PRESLEY

WILD THING IN OUTER SPACE

Dear Reg,

How are, m'dear, to lapse into your Andoverian vernacular? There has been more than one sublime moment of misunderstanding over your rich Hampshire accent when we have been talking, and none as rich as that in which I mistook your opening remark to relate to your early plumbing and building career. Phonetically it went a little like this:

Reg: 'Keith, whaaat would you sayee if oi told you oi were going to open up aholeundermisinks?'

Me: 'Say again, Reg.'

Reg: 'What would you say if I told you oi were going to open a holeundermysinks?'

Me: 'You are going to open a hole under your sink?'

Reg: 'Noooooooooo — under the Sphinx!'

It transpires that one of the eccentrics who inhabit your life is a crazed archeologist who has tapped into one of the Sphinx's paws in Egypt with some kind of audio hammer and claims to have discovered a hollowed-out chamber the size of an aircraft hanger in which he believes there is a flying saucer parked.

'Now,' you continued, nothing daunted, 'do you

think our mate Sting [you seem to have been his mate ever since I got you to play at his wedding] would like to invest in this project?'

'Certainly,' I responded promptly. 'To the best of my knowledge Sting has done nothing ridiculous with his money for a whole year. I shall inform him immediately.' I thought it best to leave your other scheme for making a substitute for petrol, which you had discovered from a medium with an Indian guide who was a direct descendant from Sitting Bull, to another time.

In American Indian mythology, you are supposed to have a lifelong responsibility for the person whom you gift with their name through life, so I suppose my having stuck you with 'Presley' when your manager Larry Page was looking for macho surnames for The Troggs, Chris 'Brittain', Ronnie 'Bond', Pete 'Staples' (never certain about that but it was his real name) has bonded us. My first sighting of The Troggs in the mid-sixties was at a club in Kingston where you played a set to three men and dog and sounded remarkably Kink-like, which was hardly surprising as Larry had previously managed them too. However, there was one number which stood out as a classic rocker and that was of course 'Wild Thing', which you took to number one in the US and here.

The simplicity and romantic appeal of a song you wrote in 1967 in fifteen minutes, after watching a Salvation army band on TV called 'The Joy String' inspired 'Love Is All Around', later the soundtrack of *Four Weddings and Funeral* in 1997 and kept Wet Wet Wet at number one for an unprecedented 15 weeks. Hopefully it has made you a millionaire, and is a lesson to all other songwriters — never sell your copyright.

There was and remains about you a wonderful

childlike awe of the world around you, and the curiosity of one who is anxious to discover more. It extends from the paranormal and things extraterrestrial to alien abductions theories. You take a great deal of these fanciful notions seriously (although God knows I have stood in enough corn circles with you to know that they are not all easily explained as hoaxes). It is also to your credit that you do not mind having your leg pulled a little.

I seem to recall that our last phone call a few months ago concerned your discovery of some book from which you are now convinced that Jesus lived on after the resurrection and had two children — one called James and another called Jesus Junior. Wonderful. Never change Reg.

The truth is out there

Keith

ELKIE
BROOKS

ELKIE
BROOKS

BEST F****** FEMALE VOCALIST

Dear Elkie,

I can recall the first time I heard your name was from the young drummer with Billy J Kramer and the Dakotas in 1963, who informed me that his fourteen-year-old cousin called Elaine Bookbinder could sing his manager Brian Epstein's latest female discovery Cilla Black 'out of her socks'. He was right.

I caught up with you at a time when your PR was being handled by my partner Chris Williams when you were singing with Vinegar Joe and the young Robert Palmer in the early seventies. Your presence in the office was usually accompanied by the air turning blue. In the sixties you possessed, and arguably still have, the best female rock and roll voice in Britain. At your best you had the passion of Janis Joplin coupled with the stage presence of Tina Turner, and your own raunchy vulgarity that could blister club wallpaper.

In the eighties, when I reinherited you as a PR for the album *Inspirations* you had sadly moved into an MOR style which seemed to dictate that you did more standards and dressed up like someone's idea of a glamorous cabaret star. Personally, I felt they should have left you alone to grow old disgracefully and be your natural feisty self, instead of trying to turn you into a TV celebrity songstress.

You could be difficult on occasion, but real talent often is — and I believed in 'Pearl's a Singer' but you can stick schmaltz-like 'Lilac Wine' on ice inspite of the great vocal. What you needed was better advice over 'club selection', as they say in golfing parlance. More driver and less wedge. I shall look forward to another mouthful of Anglo Saxon invective on our next meeting.

You too,

Keith

URIAH
HEEP

URIAH HEEP

NO ONE CAN HEAR YOU SCREAM
ON A MOUNTAIN TOP

Dear Uriah Heep,

Loved by the heavy metal fans but reviled by the critics, I had to pull some impossible scams to get you favourable publicity. Remember how we found ourselves 18,000 feet up a Swiss mountain range in a revolving restaurant, featured in the James Bond movie *On Her Majesty's Secret Service*, for your album *High and Mighty*? It was the highest restaurant in the world and the reception cost over £10,000 with a private Lear jet thrown in, piloted by your manager Gerry Bron.

You were collectively Ken Hensley (keyboards and briefcase), John Wetton (bass), Mick Box (guitar), the late David Byron (vocals) and Lee Kerslake (drums). I have to confess that most heavy metal bands, including your own, left me deafened, confused and totally underwhelmed, even though I could appreciate that individually you were talented musicians. Most of your concerts I attended as your press agent I sat out in the toilet with a good book.

However, my criteria when taking on an account were not whether I liked their music, but what the people were like I had to work with, and could I get results. Most heavy metal musicians, I have to say, were likeable, and unlike their manic performance just rock musicians in panto. The journalists who followed metal were usually far less cynical and genuine enthusiasts.

Ken Hensley, your keyboard player with waist-length hair, was a crack golfer who owned cars like a Ferrari Dino, carried a smart briefcase and took more than a passing interest in business. John Wetton was a talented bass player whom I had last seen in the group Family. Mick Box was your fast-fingered demented lead guitarist who looked like an enraged cocker spaniel on-stage, but off was quietly spoken and intelligent. The late David Byron was a hard-living but sensitive vocalist. Your drummer Lee Kerslake was a cross between Oliver Reed, Keith Moon and John Bonham.

Our mountain-top press reception was a memorable PR escapade which even gained us a column in the unlikely portals of the *Sunday Telegraph* who were understandably impressed by our being met at the Swiss airport by a man dressed as a bear which Kerslake wrestled to the ground apparently under the misapprehension it was real thus saving all our lives. The man in the bear suit waddled off in a huff.

Following the longest cable car ride in the world up the Schlithorne to the restaurant it was unfortunate that we all forgot the problems of drinking at altitude which resulted in DJ Alan Freeman collapsing and remaining for some two hours unconscious in his soup at his table while a photographer narrowly escaped death as he toppled over a ridge outside in order to find a better vantage point to photograph the group. Mr Kerslake continued his impression of the Incredible Hulk by drunkenly wrestling the manager's wife Lilian Bron to the floor under a buffet table out on the helicopter pad, apparently under the misguided notion she too was a bear. Your manager was not amused. Hours later 'Fluff' Freeman was still revolving at his table, in his soup, when your drummer decided to engage his singer David Byron in a fist fight during the cable car descent and then had to be restrained on the flight home from punching out an airplane window with his fist.

Heep trouble,

Keith

JOAN ARMATRADING

JOAN ARMATRADING

MACHO MADAM

Dear Joan,

Often sullen, bad tempered and unpredictable, you could occasionally be caught in a good mood with a smile that was sheer sunshine and St Kitts where you were born, but you had to be quick.

I recall, as with many of my eventual clients, that I interviewed you first as a journalist for *NME* in the early seventies at, of all places for such an emancipated vegetarian, the Playboy Club, where I reported your love of English comics like the *Dandy* and *Beano*, and devotion to the humour of *The Goon Show* which spawned the headline 'No one who likes Spike Milligan can be all bad.' Still remains true.

Unfortunately you were mostly memorable to me as a PR for being a kind of female equivalent of Van Morrison to work with, which should please you because you think so highly of his work. As a person, you have inherited some of Van's less loveable qualities, and your mood swings and hostility meant you were not exactly a bundle of fun to work with or represent.

However, also like Morrison, you have a compassion and originality in your work which is incomparable, and songs like 'Love and Affection', 'Mama Mercy' and 'Tall in the Saddle' are unique examples of a singular songwriter and guitarist who has deservedly sold over 4 million records worldwide.

My short tenure as your PR during the *The Key* album tour in the eighties was at least memorable for landing us both into 'Pseud's Corner' in the satirical magazine *Private Eye* over a story surrounding the metal key which you hung around your neck. As every journalist picked up on it I invented a press story which was a pseudo-intellectual send-up and attributed all kinds of derisable psychological and Freudian symbolism to the necklet with the pay-off line, 'It also happens to fit my front door and prevents my losing it.' The real explanation.

The *Eye* picked it up and missed the joke. It lopped off the debunking punch line and attributed the nonsense to you. I lamely protested to Richard Ingrams, the Editor, who went conveniently deaf and put the phone down — never liked PRs much, Ingrams, which was a pity because I loved *Private Eye*.

There seemed little doubt that you preferred the company of women, and men showing any sign of a friendly or tactile approach did so at their peril. I recall a roasting administered to me publicly backstage as your PR when I gave you an affectionate peck on the cheek in respect of a good show and you leapt into the air as though you had been stabbed with a red hot knife. 'You know I only shake hands,' you growled for the benefit of a girlfriend. I did not, but I do now.

Gertcha

Keith

OZZY
OSBOURNE

OZZY OSBOURNE

ROCK'S GREATEST LIVING MADMAN

Dear Ozzy,

I do not think there is much doubt that most of your fans who have followed the tales of your biting the heads off live bats, urinating on the steps of America's national 'shrine' at the Alamo, wandering on-stage in a frock and a Nazi helmet, hanging a dwarf as a part of the stage act ('He looks forward to it every night!') or hurling offal at the audience understandably assume you are barking mad. I did.

You certainly had a well-developed, if somewhat bizarre sense of humour, and regaled me once about the funniest film you had ever seen. 'It was *Psycho II*' you told me. 'The last scene was when Tony Perkins' mother enters and he asks if he can have some more coffee and then he smacks her over the head with a shovel and kills her. Our bass player Bob Daisley leapt to his feet in the cinema and yelled "One lump or two?"'

I actually found you to be a rather a shy and diffident character when sober, who was more interested in music than mayhem, but drunk you would turn in the kind of manic performance in keeping with the werewolf you played during the period I had your PR for the *Bark at the Moon* album.

Those around you dozed off at their own risk during recording sessions as they would awake like my assistant Roland Hyams to find that an eyebrow had been shaved off. There was also the memorable occasion when you were so out of it that you attempted to strangle your own wife Sharon, who had you committed for attempted murder before dropping the charges. She also managed you. Still happily together, I trust?

The Association of Marion Helpers in Massachusetts were so disturbed by the fact you had apparently written a song for the late devil worshipper Aleister Crowley ('I only wrote the song "Mr Crowley" because I heard about Jimmy Page living in his old house and wondered who the hell he was') that they say a mass for you every Sunday and sent you a medallion blessed by the Pope ('Very nice of em') which you wore round your neck on stage whilst hanging the dwarf.

I had done a few interviews with you in the Black Sabbath days for which you were friendly and co-operative, and I can remember your early amusement on my bewilderment watching your legendary bass player 'Geezer' Butler change from his sweaty white clinging leather stage suit into an identical dry one from a suitcase in the dressing room after the show. 'He likes to make sure he gets mobbed by the groupies as he leaves,' you explained. Magnificent.

Twenty years on you had quit Sabbath and established a reputation in the lunatic tradition of Keith Moon as the greatest living rock and roll mad man. I was dubious about taking your account after having had my problems with Moon for over a decade, but

Noddy Holder, who was a close friend of both, assured me you were just an out of control kid who could be handled. Tell that to anyone who dozed off or failed to drive into another car when you so instructed.

I had already had a brief spell looking after Sabbath minus you, and their moustachioed guitarist Toni Iommi who had memorably decked *Melody Maker* editor Allan Jones after he described you in print as 'A Jason King with builder's arms', informed me you were likeable but unpredictable.

It seemed that your failure to turn up for interviews was considered to be excusable by your office because you were 'Ozzy, for Chrissake,' but I found it inexcusable because it affected my relationship with the press and other artistes. Wasting someone's time was not funny to me or them. We sadly fell out and Roland Hyams, now a successful PR in his own right, walked out with your account. I was not ungrateful. Yet you were, as Noddy said, extremely funny and very loveable — when *sober*!

Don't ring me

Keith

SQUEEZE

SQUEEZE

RATTLE YOUR JOOLS ...

Dear Squeeze,

You were the band they predicted would be the next Beatles (a comparison equivalent in piratical terms to receiving the black spot from Blind Pew), and songwriters Chris Difford and Glenn Tilbrook were described as the next Lennon and McCartney. You had plenty of talent but absolutely no charisma. Your personality left early with Jools Holland. Someone described you cruelly as looking more like a bunch of estate agents than a band.

A talented but imageless group, you had little to capture the public's imagination and sadly very little for the media or me to exploit, but you wrote great songs.

Shame

Keith

STATUS QUO

The *Quo* with former manager Colin Johnson.

STATUS QUO

NOT SO SIMPLE

Dear Quo,

You were the band whom I most regretted losing and with whom I had most fun during the four years I represented you. Rick and Francis were the most amusing combination I have encountered off-stage or on. You were both high-octane fun and games, although sometimes it was chemically fuelled with the almost inevitable results which have caught up with Rick in recent times.

For someone so full of life and laughter as Rick Parfitt to suffer a heart attack following the tragic death of his little daughter a few years previously and a traumatic divorce from his soul mate Marietta, I can only feel the deepest sympathy. This is someone who never hurt anyone deliberately in his life, who always kept his sunny side up and probably still does.

Together with your early manager Colin Johnson you were rock and roll's answer to Wimbledon Football Club. Home grown and with a close-knit unity welded together with 'in' humour from the nucleus of John Coughlan (drums), Alan Lancaster (bass), Rick Parfitt (rhythm guitar) and Francis Rossi (lead guitar). You were forged out of adversity after two semi-psychedelic hits in the sixties with 'Pictures of Matchstick Men' and the Marty Wilde composition 'Ice in the Sun', after which you dumped the frippery of flower power and went for broke to play home-grown 12-bar blues in jeans and tee shirts.

You hammered your l2-bar blues into a rock solid structure on which you hung your own original hits whilst maintaining the impeccable harmonies, inspired by Francis' early obsession with the Everly Brothers, but never missed a beat. You kept it simple, made it sound like fun and reflected the 'party' atmosphere at your concerts on album.

Some idiots thought you sounded too repetitive and too simple to be credible, but you only made it sound simple because you had worked so long and so hard to achieve that cohesion. If it was really that simple then some other band would have done it, and no one has got close to your style. Successful simplicity is seldom easily achieved.

Internationally, your appeal was always going to be more limited because of your emphatic Englishness which, although understandable to the Europeans and Australians, never translated itself to the Americans who are notoriously resistant to rhythm and blues groups and English irony. The humour was deadpan and very Monty Python, with some cockney rhyming slang thrown in which made it incomprehensible to many Americans, although you tried your best to crack the States.

Your secret weapon was little Alan Lancaster, who was a baby-faced bass player, built like a good lightweight boxer, and when push came to shove (as it did during your memorable altercation with the airport police in Vienna) the police discovered he did not shove at all. Alan was macho and proud of it. Significantly he seemed to quit around 'Marguerita Time' on the basis of the music being unmanly and un-Quo. You tried replacing him with a cardboard cut out on *Top of the Pops*, but it never had Alan's pugnacity.

Vienna airport was already notorious in the seventies for having some over-zealous ex-fascist types on the staff who liked to give the 'long hairs' a hard time. Francis and Rick endured some manhandling following an abortive search for drugs. We knew Alan would react badly to any rough stuff in the booth. 'Nuff' had some very strong views on who could touch him and where. The first indication that Francis' warning 'not to try that on Alan' had been ignored by the security men after his 'shake down' came when a customs officer appeared to have discovered the secret of unaided flight and flew out of the curtained booth like a cruise missile, having apparently assaulted Alan's fist with his chin and thus prompting the appearance of armed police who threw the entire band and tour manager Bob Young, an onlooker, into jail.

Six months later I returned to Vienna with you for the so-called trial, and you were given a three-month sentence commuted to a heavy fine. Alan had been thrown into a cell with no beds and hardcore prisoners who proved a great deal more decent than the police. These were not nice people. We left in a hurry.

Of all the bands I handled I can remember very few who worked as hard or struggled quite so long just to forge your own identity by working in the little clubs and building from the bottom-up. You succeeded beyond your wildest dreams in England, but America was still a problem and I watched you sympathetically as you played your hearts out to a handful of fans in the Whiskey A Go Go in Los Angeles in the late sixties.

Unbeknown to you I had turned up at the club with Jim Morrison whom I had been interviewing earlier, and he left after five minutes with the words, 'Tell them to turn down, give up and go home.' I never mentioned his dispiriting advice or presence. You needed all the encouragement you could get in the U.S. and even then it would not have been enough for those who like spectacle and image instead of good solid rock and roll.

You were always generous, good hearted and good humoured, and it was humour that took you through your most difficult times. The practical jokes went on and on but one of the funniest was when we picked up journalist Nina 'The Bitch on the Box' Myscow in Ireland when she was to do an interview for the *Sun* in a rented banger with 'L' plates and Rick playing the learner driver with Francis as 'instructor'. Poor Nina was kangaroo-hopped through Cork High Street and required to get out and help push at one point whilst the 'short cut' which Rick took through a wood, as though he were participating in a high-speed rally (Rick needless to say was an experienced driver already, but Nina did not know that), resulted in her bumping her head on the roof and doors flying open, so it was more hair-raising than any roller coaster. The subsequent 'short cut' across a golf course was best deemed ill advised.

Francis was of course screaming instructions: 'Quick press the clutch ... No, No, No! The clutch, not the accelerator ... Don't put the hand brake on while we doing seventy ... brake, brake, brake! ... Those are the windscreen wipers ... Reverse! Reverse! — too late!' I must add that Nina Myscow may be regarded mistakenly by some as spiteful, but I always found her great fun and a bloody good sport while she was the showbiz editor of the *Sun*. With Quo she needed to be.

We split when I got the wrong side of a management dispute and felt I was being misrepresented. I became the fall guy, but that's showbiz, as they say, and it was my mistake. A few years ago I ran into Francis and he looked at me warily. 'You must really hate us,' he said.

'On the contrary,' I replied. 'I made a mistake and paid the penalty, but I enjoyed representing you and I miss your company.' He looked bewildered but gave me a hug and went on his way. That is the way it should be.

Be lucky

Keith

BIFF
BYFORD

Biff Byford and *Saxon*.

BIFF BYFORD

LEGEND IN HIS OWN CHAIN MAIL

Dear Biff,

By the time I became Saxon's press agent in the eighties, you had changed image from short black-haired, bearded Yorkshire tyke, to having blonde shoulder-length hair wearing white leather sequin jackets, with absurd padded shoulders and poncing about on-stage in white spandex trousers draped with metal chains which made you look like Eddy Izzard on a particularly bad dress night. With typical Barnsley candour you informed me, 'Oi loike dressing up in daft stuff on-stage — after all you got give the buggers something to look at.' Quite.

I sometimes found it difficult to cope with the brain-crunching volume which you insisted on playing at, or the mindless head-banging and body odour that seemed to accompany each barn-storming bash, but I loved the honest 'matter of fact' attitude that you all had off-stage. Maybe it was due to the fact that you got all the theatrical pretence and pantomime out of your system on-stage that you were able to relax and be real people off it.

You had an extremely gifted guitarist in Graham

Oliver who was forced to shave off his moustache because he was a dead ringer for comedian Bobby Ball, and drummer Nigel Glocher turned in sterling performances with flaming drumsticks that were sheer Spinal Tap. Perhaps most ludicrous off all was decision to promote *The Crusader* album dressed in chain mail, visors, breast-plates, visors, gauntlets and wielding two-handed broad swords.

I remember with particular fondness your staggering off-stage in armour after one performance, dripping with perspiration having screamed your chilling vocals of 'war, blood, guts, rape and pillage' only to collapse into the arms of a roadie with the request, 'Ee, oi could murder a cup of tea.' Hold the drugs.

Barnsley boys through and through, you even invited your dear old 72-year-old Dad to one performance at Sheffield Town Hall, where I spoke to him backstage and he declared he was 'reet proud of the lad'. I enquired whether thundering volume was not a bit much at his age and he said 'Oi know nothing about that — I turned moi hearing aid off.'

Your philosophy was simply that the only thing you were serious about was how you played as a band and not how you looked. 'In ten or fifteen years time I know the so-called fashionable bands like Duran Duran and Boy George will have disappeared,' you declared. 'But heavy metal acts like ours will still be around because we deliver the goods.'

Daft, I call it

Keith

RAY
DAVIES

RAY DAVIES

THE ROCK 'N' ROLL NOEL COWARD

Dear Ray,

I have always regarded you as the Noel Coward of rock and roll, and one of the most perceptive and original English songwriters of the sixties. As a person, however, your paranoia over the notion that the world was exploiting you can make things difficult. You seem to believe the rest of the world has been conspiring to part you from your money, and have adopted that old sixties maxim of, 'Do unto others what they would do unto you — but do it first and then split.'

With some justification you seem to have been enthroned as the English poet laureate of rock and roll. Your observations on the English class system are priceless little musical cameos. There is, however, a very sharp double edge to those apparently sweet little sentimental songs like 'Waterloo Sunset', 'Sunny Afternoon' and 'Dedicated Follower of Fashion'. They have a sting in the tale which makes them so intriguing. It is an extension of your own confused and complex personality which convulsively creates these coded musical knots.

A slightly fey and languid young man, I

interviewed you many times in the sixties when you could be unpredictable and sometimes spiteful, which led to spats and clashes with your younger brother Dave and other members of the band. As kid brother Dave seldom got the credit he deserved for his innovative guitar work or contributions in the recording studio. As the elder sibling you seized the initiative and realised songwriting was the key to the early power struggle. Younger brothers notoriously get a rough deal, and there was a suggestion that you had never absolved him from pushing you over as a child and causing the characteristic gap-tooth smile about which you were so sensitive as kid, but which later became a trademark and one for which you refused dental treatment when it was suggested by your manager.

Dave was an irrepressible fifteen-year-old tearaway who actually formed the first band without you, attempted physical intercourse with anything that moved and hit anything else that did not. However, he almost single-handedly invented feedback technique on guitar and, with a little more encouragement, might have had more solo hits than 'Death of a Clown'. He did not get much.

Although always quietly spoken and considered, there was a sufficient hint of menace and repressed anger in your manner which usually led to a compliment being swiftly followed by a put down. It was not long before respect turned to fear and sometimes loathing as you wielded your advantages to achieve your own ends. Your talent established you as Head Kink and spokesman.

I noted a few flashes of temper when I played in some charity soccer matches with you, and you provoked a minor tantrum in the bar at *Top of the Pops* in White City which involved your attempt to discover whether Dave Hill of Slade wore a wig and if it came off. I wrote the whole episode as 'handbags at ten paces' in *NME* and within three days received a vicious handwritten letter which I still have, threatening unpleasant things if I ever did it again.

There always seemed to be 'something of the night' and just a touch of the bully in your dealings and bass player Pete Quaife quit early on in the success story whilst drummer Mick Avory became the fall guy for you and Dave. Mick Avory's gentle, considered and lugubrious manner earned him the epithet of 'having the personality of cucumber sandwich' and being ritually humiliated. You may recall the Cucumber turned on-stage in Cardiff in the sixties and put six stitches in Dave's head with a drum pedal after kid brother publicly trashed his drum kit.

What you were unaware of was that after Mick fled on foot in fear of having killed his 'friend', with a warrant out for his arrest, he hid in my house in New Malden until the hue and cry died down and manager Larry Page persuaded him to emerge and confront his problems with the band who were due to embark on their first US tour together. A truce was effected at his office and the manager asked for any final business. Mick tentatively pointed out he would need a new drum pedal.

In common with other legendary meanies like Rod Stewart and Manfred Mann, I have an abiding memory of a conversation between you and your wife Rasa that I overheard from the front seat of the car in which we were travelling in London on one occasion in the sixties. You were already an established star and probably a millionaire on paper at least. Rasa was freezing in a little cotton dress and pleading for a coat to wear for the winter. She pleaded for some time and, to the uninitiated, you would have thought she was after a fur coat from your royalties. It eventually transpired the dispute was over your paying for her coat's return from Sketchley dry cleaners.

In the eighties I had no trouble with you during the few months that I represented you and the Kinks for a short British tour and the shooting of *Return to Waterloo* for Channel 4, although you retained that disturbing characteristic of charm and chill. I was, however, slightly thrown by Dave's declaration that he was an Arethusian. He seemed to be under the impression that Jesus was alive on Venus. Simultaneously, a German group went on record saying, 'Ray Davies is Jesus and we are all the Kinks' disciples.' So that was all right then.

There is something of the rock and roll Howard Hughes about you. For those puzzled by the plastic Tesco bag you sometimes clutch on-stage, I can reveal it is not the groceries but the cash for appearing. I would not be entirely surprised if you wound up a lonely old man with vast wealth in a huge house with one light bulb, growing your nails and wiping your fingers with Kleenex after shaking hands. Or are you already doing that?

Looking forward to the poison pen letter — I'll put it with the other one.

Kinkly

Keith

KEITH
EMERSON

KEITH EMERSON

'ELP, I NEED SOMEBODY

Dear Keith,

Sadly, I fear, you are likely to be remembered as the man who murdered Hammond organs with hunting knives, burnt the American flag at the Albert Hall, and raped synthesizers. In fact, you were a classically trained, quite brilliant keyboard player who could adapt his technique as easily to Meade Lux Lewis 'Honky Tonk Train Blues' which you took into the charts in the eighties, as you could classical pieces like Mussorgsky's 'Pictures at an Exhibition', performed with ELP.

You came out of a rhythm and blues background with Gary Farr and the T-bones, and then progressed into a progressive jazz-rock unit called The Nice which was hugely underrated but found image in the way of the music once you discovered your flair for exhibitionism and jumped astride your Hammond and rode it across the stage. As a kid you claimed to be all 'Russ Conway left hand and all Dudley More right hand', but for a while there you were the Lester Piggot of the keyboard.

With advent of Cream and Crosby Stills Nash and Young it suddenly became the age of the supergroup, and you decided to go for a group with Gregg Lake (ex-King Crimson) and Carl Palmer (ex-Atomic Rooster) that became ELP, and for a few years in the early seventies cleaned up every award including Best Group, Best Bass, Best Drummer and Best Keyboard player in the *Melody Maker* Awards. You were the progressive music punter's choice, and one time you were dragging around over seven tons, which seemed a little excessive for a trio.

Grand rock with ELP hit ludicrously grandiose levels when we hired a jet to fly us all to Japan in the seventies which was empty save for a dozen crew, and the rest of the room was taken up with the musical equipment. You played huge baseball stadiums in Tokyo and Osaka. The first took place during a typhoon called Phyliss in which you played in a dangerous electrical storm with lightning and rain lashing down under the stage canopy in the middle of a baseball diamond, with drummer Carl Palmer thrashing around like an octopus in a waterfall. The second concert in Osaka caused a full-scale riot when the 35,000 capacity audience decided they were too far from the stage and stormed the security fences and invaded the pitch, where they were met by Japanesee security forces who beat them back with ten-foot batons. I found myself abandoned on the stage, obsessed by filming the riots with my new cine camera and not noticing that everyone else had evacuated the area. I just about escaped with my life. You were outraged because the authorities turned off the power and made it impossible for you to pacify the crowd. The concert was abandoned.

Gregg was criticised for his egoism in the press, and stories of having a Persian rug to stand on-stage and his own roadie to clean it. However, he could also be considerate and kind. I recall him being the only person to realise the behaviour of our tour photographer Bob Ellis in Japan, who was running about like a man with one foot nailed to the floor screaming about not receiving co-operation. It was Gregg who deduced he was suffering from nervous exhaustion and called a doctor, after which Bob calmed down and functioned perfectly normally — for a rock photographer, that is.

You were a cool and friendly man to have a beer with, but strangely reserved and introverted on being interviewed which made you seem uncharacteristically precious. However, with a few glasses of wine, the extrovert would emerge and I loved how you solved the problem of the Japanese tourists who regularly parked in a coach outside the iron gates of the courtyard to your beautiful listed house in Sussex every Sunday, just as you were about to eat with your family. Poised to carve the Sunday joint you looked out to see the Japanese zooming in on you with their cameras from their coach parked outside. You promptly took off all your clothes, ran out the front door and did several laps of the ornamental fountain in your courtyard, waving to the abashed tourists. You were off the list of tourist attractions the following week.

Sayanora

Keith

NIK
KERSHAW

NIK KERSHAW

A RIDDLE IN HIS OWN TEEN TIME

Dear Nik,

You were one of the few enigmas amongst my clients. You wrote and performed five top-ten singles in the space of a year with 'Wouldn't It Be Good', 'I Wont Let The Sun Go Down on Me', 'Wide Boy', 'Don Quixote' and 'The Riddle'. The critics decided you were too teeny, too tiny and too temporary to be taken seriously which was imperceptive. You proved how innovative a songwriter you were by turning in another number one for Chesney Hawkes in with 'The One and Only' in 1991, and he made a huge error by not going for another of your songs as a follow up and disappeared.

You had a shrewd manager in Mickey Modern, who believed in your long-term talent, and a good record company in MCA. Everything seemed to be in gear but you never quite shook off the teeny idol image. You seem to have everything but ruthlessness. You became swiftly bored with the screaming and uncomfortable as a married man with the teenage adulation. The wife was another problem and you were not the first person to have one who was resented by the business — Yoko and the late Linda McCartney suffered from that problem, but their respective partners were hugely successful and could ride out the criticism. Sheri became too obvious too soon, and did not always have the common sense to know when it was sensible to retire to a neutral corner. One unwritten law in life and showbusiness is do not come between husband and wife, and it angered you every time someone did. You had a genuine relationship and were not prepared to jeapordise it, but sometimes discretion is essential — especially when the other lover is Fame, who is extremely jealous.

Sheri was a good, supportive wife, but intrusive and it became a management issue. You instictively knew how to play the game. She did not and resented being sidelined. How do you tell someone their wife is not a public relations asset? Extremely carefully is the answer.

I inherited you when you had already been launched as one of the teen screams of the eighties and like most others you hated it after the first novelty had worn off. There was absolutely no reason why you should not have emerged from the teen infatuation like George Michael, Sting and Robbie Williams. You wrote arguably the most original pop song of the eighties called 'The Riddle'. Elton went on record as declaring you one of the most talented songwriters to emerge in the nineties. He was right.

Regards to 'Her Outdoors',

Keith

LEO
SAYER

Leo Sayer with
Keith and Keith's
son Bryan.

LEO SAYER

THE MOUSE THAT ROARED

Dear Leo,

You were unfortunately a first-class little clown who could not resist playing the fool and destroying your own credibility. It was Adam Faith who dragged me down to Brighton to see you in a band called Patches in the early seventies, discovered by him and his partner Dave Courtney. I wrote the first major piece on you in a music paper before you had even released a record. You had potential rock star written all over your cute curly head, and a magnificent bluesy-falsetto range which put you in a class of your own.

I wrote a piece on you in *NME* predicting great things and introduced you to Roger Daltrey who recorded an entire solo album of your songs and scored a hit with your song 'Giving it all Away'. You were off and running, although now more obviously pop star than rock star. Adam hit on the device of hiding some of your more over-the-top tendencies behind the white make-up of the traditional circus clown. It was a master stroke because it gave you mystery and gravitas. No one could penetrate the disguise at first and find the comedian.

I suspect that Adam secretly knew all along that it was pointless trying to turn a wannabe, an all-round entertainer, into a rock star of substance and simply wiped off the make-up and gave you your head as a solo entity. For a while the great voice and good compositions like 'The Show Must Go On', 'Moonlighting', 'You Make Me Feel Like Dancing', 'More Than I Can Say' and covers like 'When I Need You' kept you in the top ten, but the kids grow swiftly tired of someone with a superficial attitude.

By the time I inherited your publicity most of your 'rock' credibility was out the window, and Adam had made a mistake by splitting from your co-writer and mentor Dave Courtney and going for broke with the TV cabaret star route that you seemed determined to follow. It was sad to see you with Reeves and Mortimer recently on TV being encouraged to make a monkey out of yourself whilst piggie backing and singing your big hit as Bob bore you on a running machine. You were always up for it.

Shame, because you had enormous potential, but you made some real bad moves and agreed to some worse ones. I regret to say the business made a mug out of you with your help.

Send in the clown,

Keith

ANGUS
YOUNG

ANGUS YOUNG

A HOT ROCK 'JUST WILLIAM'

Dear Angus,

I seem to recall that it was General Noreiaga ('Old Pineapple Face'), the Pan American dictator, who was finally driven from hiding in the nineties by the liberators playing AC/DC tapes at excruciating high volume directed at his palace retreat. He surrendered, emerging defiant but deaf.

I inherited your press in the nineties based on a previous association with your manager for whom I publicised ELP in the eighties. Stuart Young was known to employees as 'Mr Sunshine' due to his unjolly disposition, but there was nothing miserable about you or the band who were high-octane fun and games. An interesting mix of original Aussies and press-ganged Brits.

You had a good act with the demon schoolboy image you had evolved for the stage and were no mean guitarist on the run. No one ever seemed to discover why you had taken to the schoolboy cap and short trousers, but as a diminutive figure I am sure you had your fair share of 'Get Shorty' jokes back home in Australia and decided to make a strength out of adversity.

There was plenty of the response to your boyish

Australian image and pithy comments in the music press like *NME* who wrote: 'They're not poofs, and have huge great bloody amplifiers to prove it,' whilst your brother Malcolm declared manfully, 'A lot of our songs have double meanings — but you've got to cover up the filth somehow.' I could never quite understand why you seemed to regard 'mooning' with your backside to the audience to be necessary, but there you go.

One music critic wrote ambiguously of your UK tour, 'To castigate AC/DC for sexism is a bit like castrating your dog for trying to shag someone else's leg,' whilst *Melody Maker* described you as sounding like 'a clogged artery pulsing'. Another critic wrote he would 'no more go to an AC/DC concert than sniff a dead skunk.' Fair does.

Those who came to Wembley Arena to see you on 'The Razor's Edge' tour I publicised saw one of the tightest rock and roll bands I had heard since The Who when Keith Moon was at his best in the band. You are a dynamite little guitarist on the move and the more the press slated you, the more the kids loved you. Brian Johnson, your aimiable Geordie vocalist with a voice that sounded like he gargled with gravel, had an ingenious solution for some critics. 'I'd like to lock them up in cell with our new album for a week. Then I'd pump in a week's worth of disco music and I bet you pound to a pinch of shit they'd be found hanging by their own belts. With AC/DC at least they come out humming the choruses.'

You were too good to be just deemed heavy metal and 'Thunderstruck' was one of the best rock and roll singles I have ever heard. Good lads. No probs.

G'day

Keith

254

JIMI
HENDRIX

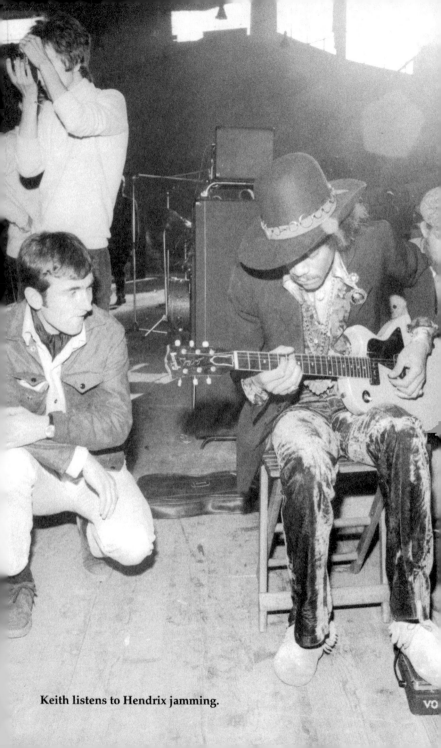

Keith listens to Hendrix jamming.

JIMI HENDRIX

KING GUITAR

Dear Jimi,

I hope you're up there giggling somewhere and still loping around playing, clasping and cuddling your guitar. It was often said you would have intercourse with the damn thing if you could, and I recall watching you wander around your London flat whilst making breakfast wearing it as if it were just another limb. Your guitar was like a third arm — which some jealous guitarists thought you had anyway.

Somewhere I have one of your guitar straps which you gave me as a belt when we were go-karting in Majorca prior to a gig. I must get it valued sometime — not that I would dream of selling it. You would be pleased to see your bass player Noel Redding's house in Ireland now which is a shrine to the Experience memory, and he still has a tear in his eye when he talks about you. You hurt him badly replacing him without warning on an American tour.

Amongst my minor claims to fame is that I was the man who came up with the idea of you setting fire to your guitar on-stage, and I completed the last interview with you just three days prior to your death. I made my first trip to America with you in 1966 for the Monterey Festival at which you made your American debut, introduced by Brian Jones, where your flaming guitar stole the show from Otis Redding, Janis Joplin, The Mama and the Papas, Steve Miller, Neil Young, Steven Stills and The Who.

I trust your manager, my friend the late Chas Chandler, is also 'up there' giving you a hard time for running around with the dealers, druggies and dopers that leeched on to you after you split from him following the 'glory albums' he produced like *Are You Experienced?*, *Axis Bold As Love* and *Electric Ladyland*. If you had only returned to him sooner, as you planned, you might still be with us. Chas was your real mentor, and the one record producer capable of extracting your diamond-like moments of inspiration in the studio, which often came from hours of indulgent jamming and improvisation You desperately needed someone brave enough to edit your indulgences or tell you when to stop. When Chas quit because he could no longer bear the parasites and hangers-on which surrounded you in New York, you lost the one adviser who would tell you the truth.

Legend has it that Chas first met you at the Cafe Wha after a tip-off from Keith Richard's girlfriend Linda. Keith and the Rolling Stones manager, Andrew Oldham, had turned you down pronouncing 'guitarists never happen', thus eclipsing even Auntie Mimi's immortal advice to the teenage John Lennon at her home in Liverpool that, 'A guitar is all very nice, John, but you will never make a living with it.'

You revealed to me that you remembered meeting Chas years before he discovered you playing in New York, in an elevator in Seattle. He was still playing bass with the Animals when he went to see his friend Tony

Hicks of the Hollies on a TV spectacular in which you were also appearing as Little Richard's guitarist. Richard threw a tantrum in the elevator and a security guard decided to examine his nostrils with the barrel of his gun, at which point you and Chas bailed out on the first available level and left them screaming at each other. You sat on a window sill and chatted about the Animals and shared a joint. You had your hair waxed back and were wearing a tuxedo, so it was hardly surprising he failed to remember you later.

Due to my close friendship with Chas from his days with the Animals, he asked my advice as to how he should launch you on arrival in the UK. I told him that if you were as good as he said you were, then all he had to do was to get you seen and heard. He sold his treasured guitars to enable you to stay in England. He was a good man. Early on, Chas had a few strange ideas about suiting and booting you, which I tried to discourage because I sensed, after meeting you for the first time, that you were into new looks. After working with the flamboyant Little Richard you had ideas of your own about dress, and loved the lurid colours of the psychedelic scene in London, so you wanted to give the lurid colours, scarves and fancy pants an airing.

There was one significantly funny story you told me about working with 'The Queen of Rock' on tour in America when you turned up for work in a bright yellow ruffled shirt. 'Little Richard just turned up at rehearsal, took one look at my new shirt and screamed, "Sheeet — there's only room for one pretty thing on this stage and The Georgia Peach is here to stay — you fired!" He re-hired me next day after I sold the shirt. Next week I got fired again for missing the band bus.'

When Little Richard toured England years later, while you were still struggling for a hit, you visited him at his London hotel and claimed that he owed you a week's wages. Richard's eyes bulged and he pointed at you accusingly. 'You missed the bus you rascal,' he retorted and refused to cough up. Chas initially bought a highly expensive formal stage suit out of his rapidly dwindling savings as he sought to improve your image, and you told me embarrassedly later that 'its not my thing' but you did not want to hurt his feelings. I suggested you do what the Rolling Stones did when Andrew Oldham tried to get them into stage suits. They wore them once and conveniently lost them. 'You mean deliberate?' you asked.

'Yes,' I said.

'Damn,' you replied. 'I could never do that.' But the suit mysteriously disappeared.

Once I turned up to interview you at Chas' office in London for *Rave* magazine and you were clad in a wonderful old military jacket acquired from the trendy boutique Lord Kitchener's Valet. We cooked up a publicity story about some veterans claiming that you were degrading the uniform, but you were abashed to discover later that it was the jacket of a non-combatant veterinary surgeon who looked after the donkeys which pulled the cannons. 'Still, I have had the shit end of things most of my life too,' you said. 'So maybe it's the right thing.'

I had heard you play your first brilliant jam at the London Speakeasy club weeks previously, where The Who's manager Kit Lambert trampled all over John Lennon as he stomped over the diners' tables to reach Chas and make him sign an agreement on a table napkin for his Track Records label. I confessed to Chas initially I thought you might be too clever to be appreciated commercially and, like the great jazz trumpeter Miles Davis, you could go straight over the heads of the pop market. 'Not while I'm his manager,' said Chas emphatically.

Once the Stones, the Beatles, The Who and Clapton had seen and heard how the guitar played you and you played the guitar, the word spread like wildfire about your brilliant technique. All you needed was a hit single. Chas hyped your first single 'Hey Joe' into the lower reaches of the *NME* chart, and once it was established as chart play material it took off by its own volition. But you really had to be seen to be believed.

Of all the things written about you since your death, perhaps the one thing which most commentators miss in view of your genius was that you were great fun as a person, although some of your waspish responses were often lost on reporters who missed the softly whispered retorts, when your incredibly long fingers fluttered nervously to your lips and you tailed off with 'etcetera, etcetera, etcetera,' after realising the interviewer had missed the point. You were similarly stinging with your stage introductions in foreign countries where you knew they would not catch what you were saying, and sometimes you treated a show like a rehearsal. On-stage in Zurich I can recall, 'Here's something else you won't appreciate or care about,' and 'We would like to do something ... like go home now, but hell you'd probably just follow us.' That was the show for which I was on a plane with Stevie Winwood, Eric Burdon, John Mayall, The Move and The Koobas.

One of your best one-liners occurred prior to your being invited to jam with your great rival Eric Clapton and Cream at the London Polytechnic. I asked you how you rated him you said: 'He is a kinda hero of mine, except I don't really have heroes, but I can't wait to find out if he is as good as he really thinks I am.' You looked slyly out your manager's window in Gerrard Street.

The bounds of credulity were really stretched when your first English tour found you on a pop package tour with the Walker Brothers, Engelbert Humperdinck and good old Cat Stevens — who could bore the pants off anyone with his attempts to imbue 'Matthew and Son' with social significance, although 'Gotta Get Me a Gun' was much enlivened on-stage by your drummer Mitch Mitchell, who accompanied him on the back of the head from the wings with a water pistol.

'This is a silly little tour,' you admitted during an interview with me for *NME*. 'I go on and tear up the stage so the audience are jumping up and down and then on comes Engelfluff and stops the show dead with "The Last Waltz", and damn me if that Scott Walker follows that by being even more miserable. He is so pretty and so sad that every time I run into him I want to kiss him and make it feel better. You got some great artistes here, but they are too squeaky clean and they have to stop looking at arrangements all the time. Good music comes from deep inside.'

When we flew out of Heathrow Airport for the Monterey Festival in 1966, I was not prepared for the prejudice and problems your appearance was going to cause when we landed in New York *en route*. In those days there was a difficulty getting a cab in the Village if you looked like a hippie, had long hair or were a poor black. You managed to make it on all three counts, and I had to hide you in shop doorways to get a cab — even then we had trouble as they would try to run you over.

We managed to find the original 'cabbie from hell' on the first try in downtown New York, who was the archetypal Brooklyn driver of the era with an unlit cigar stub between his teeth, baseball match on the radio, and everything he said sounded like 'toirdyturdanturdstreet' to me. You and I bundled into the back of the cab and I told the driver we were going to the Chelsea Hotel. 'Wots dat piece a shit doin in da back of ma cab?' came the response. Like an idiot I turned to see what he was talking about and could only see you turned to stone in your black hat and red frilled shirt. 'Dat piece a shit in the girlies hat,' volunteered our worthy driver. 'Get it out of my cab.'

It finally dawned on me he was talking about you, and I volunteered an observation on his parentage and that he should now drive us to the nearest cop shop where we could have a meaningful discussion about civil rights and race relations. You, meanwhile, were roundly cussing me and pulling me out of the cab. Once the human arsehole had driven off you explained I was never to do anything like that again. 'I have been soaking up shit like that all my life,' you said. 'I know how to handle it and you do not — don't do it. Did you see his gun? Of course not. Well I did. I thank you Keith, but no thank you. Leave it to me. One day that kind of person is going to grovel and take me anywhere I want for free.'

Two years and a few million album sales later I flew into New York to do an interview with you whilst you were recording at your Electric Ladyland Studio. I was put through to your apartment by an ultra polite receptionist who informed me, 'I have Mr Hendrix on the line for you.'

'You hear that Keith?' you laughed. 'Mister Hendrix. I'm not the nigger in the silly hat any more — I am Mr Hendrix in New York and they treat me with respect.'

It seemed like your problems with cab drivers were not over, though, because we got one later who begged to come to the studio with his kit and just play for free with you. Being the soft-hearted touch you were you mumbled 'sometime', and two hours later he turned up at the studio with a complete drum kit and set up. He was the worst drummer we had ever heard and it took two days to get him out the studio. 'What can you do?' you said. 'He went all the way back to the Bronx to get his kit.'

I have a feeling it might amuse the hell out of you that after thirty-five years in the music business as a press agent to the Stones, Sting, the Beach Boys and The Who, amongst others, that one of my main claims to fame in music books is as the man who gave you the idea of setting your guitar on fire. There I am immortalised in *'Scuse Me While I Kiss the Sky* by David Hendersen (page 114), *Are You Experienced* by Noel Redding (page 47), and the estimable *Crosstown Traffic* by Chas Shaar Murray (page 45), as the man who flambéd Hendrix's guitar.

The guitar flambé was created on the opening night of that 'silly tour' when Chas, road manager Gerry Stickles and I were plotting what we might do to steal the thunder from the Walker Brothers who were headlining the show. Chas thought you needed a stunt and asked my advice. 'The Who are doing auto-destruction to death, so you can't just smash a guitar,' I said. 'And The Move have even taken an axe to a TV set on-stage.'

'Mebbe I could smash up an elephant,' you mumbled. 'It's a pity you can't set fire to your guitar,' I suggested, 'But of course, a solid state head would never burn.'

There was a significant pause while we watched the wheels going round in Chas' head, and finally he said to Stickles, 'Gerry go out and buy some lighter fuel — it will burn like a torch on the surface.'

'How about me?' you initially asked, but gradually became over-enthusiastic about setting fire to the

Walker Brothers and keen to start the next Great Fire of London. Your guitar first burst into flames halfway through 'Wild Thing' on-stage at the Finsbury Park Astoria on March 3lst 1966 after I had watched you make two desperate attempts to light it with matches. You finally got off your knees and arose to whirl the flaming instrument around your head, thus enraging the fire security officer who was not mollified with the excuse later that you were trying to put it out by this method.

There was an amusing after bonfire cameo when your agent who ironically rejoiced in the name of Tito Burns, to whom you were devoted as he had once confessed that he started out as a music-hall act with an accordion and a monkey, came backstage to give you a mock dressing down. 'What is more, you will never work on this circuit again,' shouted Tito as he flounced from the dressing room in his ankle-length, cream raincoat out of which you could just see the neck of your charred guitar, which he spirited away before it could be used as incriminating evidence. The fire chief was distinctly unamused, but of course it captured the headlines and became something everyone claimed to have seen you do on-stage, although curiously you only performed the conflagration on three occasions.

I recently ran into the man who was once the greatest footballer in the world — George Best — in the New King's Road and reminded him of the good times we all had in Majorca at the opening of Chas' 'Sergeant Pepper Club' where you played a blistering set with the Experience and literally bought the ceiling down with the neck of your guitar — much to Chas' embarrassment as he had just spend £25,000 putting it up. I reminded George of some of our nights out together, and how I pestered him with silly questions like how he felt when he scored that magnificent goal which helped win the European Cup for Manchester United in the sixties.

'I'm sorry,' said George politely, 'but I don't remember you. But I sure as hell remember Jimi Hendrix.'

Legend has you down as the wildman of rock, but in person you were a gentle soul, despite some of the heated arguments with your long-term English girlfriend Kathy Etchingham. At least she maintains you were never physically violent with her. Some other females sadly still carried bruises from encounters of the less gentle kind. You had an almost childlike naivety about being able to cope with the drugs and low life who inevitably turn up to ride a rock and roll gravy train. You were never assertive enough to resist temptation or cope with the 'The Black Panthers' or devious mafia-like heavies in New York, so it was inevitable that a man who could not say no would be vulnerable when Chas walked away from the circus, declaring it was either them or him.

At one point when you got a little 'difficult' it was even rumoured that your late manager Mike Jeffries staged a kidnapping in New York which left you in a locked basement for several days before faking the rescue themselves to earn your gratitude. Three days before your death I completed the last interview with you at the Cumberland Hotel in London, and you had re-met with Chas and were full of plans for the future which included him producing your next album.

Following your tragic overdose, all kinds of weird conspiracy theories have emerged, none of which bear close examination. There was the 'last phone call' when you allegedly left a message on Chas' answerphone that night saying, 'Please help me.' I know that was untrue because Chas had no answerphone, and there was another untrue story about a whole squad of people who were supposed to have been in the flat with your girlfriend Monika.

The truth about your death was tragic but simple. You were a massively talented, lovable but weak character who made an error of judgement over drugs and died — it was not the first time in the dirty business of dreams, and it will sadly not be the last. You could never say no, you sadly never seemed to find anything to stand for, and so you fell for everything.

There is no great sin in becoming an addict — it is just stupid.

What a tragic loss.

Keith

SMALL
FACES

SMALL FACES

TINY TALENT — BIG HEARTS

Dear Small Faces,

When my grandfather, another 'Charlie Watts', used to say, 'Never frighten a little guy — he may kill you,' he must have had you four in mind as the most formidable group of talented little musicians I have encountered. This is a sad epistle to have to address to just two remaining members, Kenny Jones (drums) and Ian McLagan (keyboards) now that your two great songwriters Steve Marriott and Ronnie Lane are gone. Steve tragically died in a fire at his home a few years ago, and Ronnie Lane from a long battle with multiple sclerosis in Texas.

I represented Steve for four years right through his supergroup days with Humble Pie in the seventies, and Kenny Jones in the eighties when he deputized for Keith Moon after his death and later formed a group with Paul Rodgers called The Law in the nineties. I also worked for Ronnie and Pete Townshend on their underrated album *Rough Mix*, and Ronnie on a number of solo projects including the 'Arms' tour.

It is worth mentioning that the 'Arms' tour started

out when Ian Stewart and I had the idea of asking the goodhearted Jeff Beck at his birthday party in 1983 if he would put together a band for a one-off concert at Hammersmith Odeon to raise some money to help fund Ronnie's medical treatment. Clapton overheard and promptly volunteered his services, and before we knew it we also collected a bunch of 'good guys' like Jimmy Page, Stevie Winwood, Ray Cooper, Charlie Watts, Bill Wyman, Andy Fairweather-Low and Chris Stainton. Ronnie was delighted, but not for himself. He promptly turned it into a world tour to raise money for all the sufferers from MS, and refused to receive a penny personally. Typical of a 'Little Big Heart'.

Ian McLagan was the only SF I did not publicise, but we were sufficiently good mates for him to put me up in LA for a few days in the nineties. I talked to his wife Kim who was Keith Moon's ex-wife, about a film on her ex-husband's life being planned by Roger Daltrey. Still planned.

Marriott was your main creative force and the 'Imposer' for any group he worked with as his funny, cocky and impulsive style impelled him to dominate. But he by no means got it all his own way with the considerable pugnacity around him. I saw him walk out on the rest of you at Crystal Palace one night after equipment difficulties in the late sixties and never come back. Steve was talented, selfish, funny, lovable, assertive and capricious in that order. When you consider that at fourteen he had already appeared in Lionel Bart's *Oliver* as the Artful Dodger, and made cameo film appearances with Peter Sellers and David Hemmings as a child actor in potboilers like *Live It Up*, it was hardly surprising he was also precocious.

He first turned up at the age of fifteen in my office

at IPC magazines in 1962 under the guise of messenger boy from manager/publicist Tony Calder, and refused to leave until I told him all about the Shadows and Cliff for whom I was writing a disc column. He was all balls and bullshit even as a teenager. He idolised the Shadows and formed an early group called the Moments who did copy-cat Shadows hits.

He loved risk and those who sailed close to the wind made the game more exciting for him. You managed to collect three of the most notorious managers in rock music over the years in Don Arden, who later managed ELO and Black Sabbath, and then Andrew Oldham who managed the Rolling Stones, and finally American Dee Anthony who had previously managed Tony Bennett and Ten Years After. You knew that anyone who managed you or the group would have to be tough because at the first opportunity you would career off the rails.

The Small Faces were always ahead of the game as a group, and with just a little more luck and some better direction you would have joined the other sixties groups breaking America at the time. But often the infectious humour of the music did not translate overseas, and no one individual seemed to have the appeal necessary for an American teenage idol.

Although the group war cry in the sixties was 'Nuf, Nis and Reeb' (spell them backwards), the early Small Faces success in the UK — with massive hits like 'All or Nothing', 'Tin Solder', 'Itchycoo Park' and 'Lazy Sunday' were never enough for Steve because he always wanted to emulate the Beatles and the Stones as a world force. When your mini masterpiece *Ogden's Nut Gone Flake* (the first rock album in a circular sleeve) failed to chart high in the US, he calculated the way forward was the supergroup. He formed Humble Pie with Peter Frampton, Greg Ridley and Jerry Shirley leaving the Faces to fall into the clutches of Rod Stewart. It worked for Steve for a while in America with some bestselling albums like *Smokin'*, but he wound up eating Humble Pie in the end. `

As the Faces, Kenny, Mac and Ronnie did extremely well until Rod Stewart got a touch of the 'Big I Ams' and sloped off in the general direction of Hollywood to further his solo career. Ronnie had already seen the writing on the wall and formed his own band with the apt name Slim Chance. Just how highly rated Kenny was as a drummer became obvious when he was selected by The Who to replace Keith Moon. McLagen's dexterity on the keyboards got him regular stints with Bob Dylan, Bruce Springsteen and The Rolling Stones.

Steve's death was a tragic accident, but at least I was able to see him a few months before, playing a typically 'ballsy' gig with The Steve Marriott Band at our local hall in Ewell, still using that big voice from that little frame with such effect. He came back to my house for a few beers afterwards and suddenly asked, 'When did you lose yours then?' I realised he was talking about my considerably reduced thatch, and announced that his was a wig, which I had not realised. The complete tea cozy, bless him. With or without hair you were some talent, sunshine.

Ronnie Lane fell in love with the Romany way of life from the days when he used to bunk off school to work for the travelling fairs which graced our English village greens. He would ride the bumper cars collecting the fares. He loved that whole concept of travelling and moving on which went with the gipsy way of life, and even tried to incorporate it into his

'Travelling Show' in the eighties which featured entertainers, circus acts and musicians. It lost him a fortune in bad weather when people are less inclined to sit in a huge, cold, wet tent. Ronnie loved the whole muddy mess. His supporting cast quit in droves.

Ronnie's personal tragedy was of course the onset of MS, which he fought courageously for many years and sought any possible cure, no matter how bizarre, including the oxygen pressure chambers which divers used. He even radically installed himself in the Rattlesnake Venom Clinic in Miami where Ian Stewart of the Stones and I went to visit him in the eighties, to find him putting on a brave face over his treatment. 'I can't say I have noticed any dramatic improvement,' he said, 'but there is a beneficial side effect, because if a mosquito bites me now it dies instantly.' Brave and immensely lovable little Ronnie seemed just to fade away and die in the middle of Texas, where not even his close friends had any details of a funeral.

Kenny Jones was something of a revelation later when I represented him in my capacity as The Who's press agent. He had developed a keen business sense, and a capacity for not being a victim which probably stemmed from having to cope with Steve Marriott and later The Who. I always thought he was harshly treated by The Who when they decided after a few years that perhaps you were not the right man to fill Moon's boots — as though anyone could.

You had another crack with that fabulous vocalist Paul Rodgers from Free when you formed The Law, but long-distance management from America was a problem and you seemed to suffer from the right advice. You are a gutsy little bloke and a powerful percussionist who has now appointed yourself 'chief investigator' into SF's early royalties. My money is on you ferreting it out successfully, because you do not quit on anyone or anything.

'Nuf, nis and reeb,' lads

Keith

MARC
BOLAN

MARC BOLAN

THE LITTLE BOPPER

Dear Marc,

You were a friend, and one of my favourite clients for over five years until your tragic death in a car crash. You were generous, good-humoured, egotistical, intuitively brilliant, conceited, extremely lovable, narcissistic, self-destructive, sexually confused, arrogant, disturbingly talented and capriciously inspired. You were also the most endearing and best-loved by your fans of all the artistes I ever represented. You genuinely loved the kids who often camped out all night long in the office doorways across from your management offices in New Bond Street, and sent over food and drink for them during their all-night vigils. You never forgot the 'Bolanites'.

'When the kids stop coming I might as well pack it in, Keith. They bought "Hot Love", "Telegram Sam" and "Get It On", and because of them I can afford to do just what I like,' you once told me, bizarrely astride a huge wooden rocking horse, in front of a picture window, overlooking the fans gathered in the doorway one summer afternoon in 1973.

It was best termed 'ill-timed' that Alfie O'Leary who

was also your driver, 'nurse' and close friend should be dismissed just a few weeks before your fateful car crash. It has often been mooted that if Alfie had still been in charge at the time you might still alive. He now does just as caring and loyal a job for Eric Clapton.

It seemed inevitable to me that a pop star who wore make-up like Rudolph Valentino to 'emphasise my good points', owned a Siamese cat called 'Flook', relied upon a fairy-muse called 'Poon' whom you claimed lived on your mantlepiece, kept a white mouse called 'Boink', sired a child called Rolan Bolan, was best friends with 'Guy the Gorilla' in London Zoo, wrote four number-one hit records and eleven top-ten hits in under three years, coined the phrase 'never trust anyone over thirty' and promptly died aged twenty-nine, would become the legend he always predicted he would do from the age of eight. Today you are numbered amongst the Top Twenty Most Collectable Artistes in the World, and your early recordings and memorabilia sell for tens of thousands of pounds. You notched up over 20 consecutive hit singles, 10 albums and over 50 million records worldwide. Ex-Beatle Ringo Starr directed a 'rockumentary' movie about you titled *Born to Boogie* at the height of Bolanmania which broke box office records throughout the UK. Ten million record sales in Japan alone, and another l2 million in the US testify to your international success.

Just a few days before your death you arrived at my office in Victoria to meet David Rooney, a dedicated fan from Birmingham who had plans for helping you consolidate the various factions of your fan clubs and magazines. As usual I had the task of vetting him, and decided he was both genuine and committed and might prove very useful. You were completing a series of press interviews in my office, but were dubious when it came to meeting David. I insisted you had promised, and the boy would be desolated.

'Just a few minutes then,' you sighed, 'Wheel him in.'

The young fan entered the office sporting a 'Marc Bolan is God' badge which immediately endeared him to one who was not immune to flattery. You both got on so well that you spent several hours with David, took him on a tour of London in your chauffeur-driven Bentley to Buckingham Palace, and out for lunch at Langan's restaurant.

Speaking to me on the phone next morning, sadly for the last time, you said you were taken with the idea of uniting all your fan clubs and had agreed to play at the grand fan club gathering where you were going to enlist the co-operation of your ex-sidemen and your common-law wife Gloria Jones. 'Gloria could warm them up with a few songs and we might become one huge family,' you prattled and amazingly added, 'Perhaps June might help.' June Bolan was your long suffering ex-wife whom you seldom if ever referred to in the last years — you liked to give the impression of being rejected and abandoned, although in reality the break-up was largely the fault of your own fickleness.

I felt, as your press agent, that you were about to make a phoenix-like surge from the ashes of the tubby little gone-to-seed glam rocker you had lately been described as by the press. You were cruelly described by one as now looking like a 'glittering chipolata' on-stage. It hit home and you came off the booze and began exercising. You looked slim, healthier and some of the old intuition and fervour had returned.

You played me a curious collaboration with David Bowie called 'Madman' at you home in Sheen which indicated a switch in direction to an electric *avant-garde* rock style which sounded like Stockhausen meets Brian Eno. Everything was pointing to a successful comeback for you, but five days later you were dead.

On Friday, September 16th 1977 at approximately 4.30 a.m. I was awoken at my home in Epsom by a call from the Press Association informing me that your car, driven by Gloria with you in the back, had crashed into a tree in Rocks Lane, Barnes and you were dead. I was shattered. 'Do you have photo of them both together?' asked the man from the PA.

Weirdly, you believed from the age of eight that you were destined to become a star and that like James Dean you would die young. The devotion of your fans is still testified by the gaily-coloured scarfs, ribbons and bows which to this day decorate the tree in Barnes into which they believe you crashed. I pass it nearly every day. In fact the actual tree was so damaged the council removed it years ago.

As a kid in the late sixties you would plague the life out of music journalists like myself in pubs like the Brewmaster above Leicester Square Station where you pleaded with us to write something about you in *NME*, *Disc*, *Melody Maker* or *Record Mirror*. You were fifteen and had not even released a record, but had inveigled yourself in to the photo pages of *Town* magazine as a young mod model adopting their dress sense and style. You were no more a mod than David Bowie, but were always prepared to be anything to anybody to get noticed. You could sniff a new fashion or trend ahead of the pack, and were a chancer, but you also had unnerving charm and self-confidence. 'You guys will regret not writing about me one day. You'll see one day I will be more popular than Presley and bigger than the Beatles and ...'

'Sure, Marc, let us know when you make a record

and you're old enough to buy a drink. Meanwhile, have a coke, sit down and shut up,' was the sort of short shrift we fogeys in our early twenties gave you for infiltrating our drinking school with the big boys like Keith Moon, Eric Burdon and Allan Clarke of the Hollies.

There was something disturbing in you believing so obsessively in your own destiny. You had an unshakeable belief and confidence in your inevitable success. As a songwriter you were one of those sensitively-tuned young people who could receive the feelings and moods of a generation and bounce them back. You made yourself a perfect mirror of glam rock and the flower power generation. You also periodically claimed to be bisexual when it suited you and seemed prepared to give anything a go if it advanced your career, you empathised with Brando's famous retort in *The Wild One* who, when asked, 'What are you rebelling against?' responded enigmatically, 'What have you got?'

'I sometimes wish I were a hundred per cent gay,' you said tweefully years later. 'It would be much easier, but not much more fun. Anyway, I checked it out when I was younger and I like boobs and prefer chicks.'

What you most certainly understood was that it was more interesting to the media and record buyers in the seventies to adopt an androgynous style even if you were predominantly heterosexual. Early Jagger had already cashed in on a bisexual image, and Bowie was turning it into an art form. You saw it more as a curiosity and a business opportunity.

Your first flower power album title was a masterpiece of hippyness called *My People Were Fair And Had Sky In Their Hair ... But Now They're Content To Wear Stars On Their Brows* which struck a chord with those looking for inner truth and able to ignore brutal reality.

You latched on to the sound of words and the feelings of the times — you were a natural receiver and reflector. You absorbed the mood of the moment and mirrored it for those who were similarly entangled in their own emotional caprice.

Your early songs were specifically honed for the flower power generation and produced some magnificently pretentious titles like 'Prophets, Seers and Sages', 'The Angel of the Ages', 'The Beard of Stars', 'Beginning of Doves' and 'Blessed Wild Apple Girl', most of which featured you and Steve 'Peregrine' Took bleating like a couple of lambs about to burst into tears.

You loved the sound of words, 'tone poems' as you called them, and your dyslexia meant your ear was even more acutely attuned to their sound. I still have a number of your letters that you wrote to me for the purpose of inclusion in a column that I wrote for *Record Mirror* in your name, and although perceptive they were almost illiterate. Your secret was simple. You just followed heart and led with your chin whilst proclaiming long and loud that you were the greatest.

Whilst you flitted like a musical magpie amongst the gems of hippy literature from Gibran to Tolkein to Hesse with a liberal sprinkling of Michael Moorcock, the spangled spectre of glam rock was on the horizon and the little chameleon was changing colours again. I interviewed you at the Albert Hall for *NME* with Took, and congratulated you on the rapid improvement of your guitar playing. 'Still ain't no Jimi Hendrix,' you grinned and playfully pretended to set fire to your guitar with a match in one corner of the dressing room. You knew I had come up that scam.

When I took over your publicity in 1972 you were already estranged from your wife June, whom I had met on innumerable occasions as a journalist. June was a tower of strength to you in your early career and provided much-needed backbone when she worked for Blackhill Enterprises, and you shared those hard times in the cold-water flat in Blenheim Crescent making love in the back of the little van parked on the edge of Wimbledon Common.

June loved and believed in you from the start when you were nothing — she was instantly struck by your appearance and sexual magnetism, although she considered herself immune from the normal come-ons inherent in a pop star.

She became your unofficial tour manager and roadie for Tyrannosaurus Rex, lending her support, encouragement and sorting the early bills and receipts. She also helped him keep your feet on the ground, and lent common sense to your more outrageous schemes. 'Hey, you know that John Lennon wants to produce me ... David Bowie and I are going to do a new concept album about the beginning of the Universe ... Jack Nicholson and I are going to star in a major movie which I am writing ... I am going to star in stage musical about the early life of James Dean ... I am going to produce the Damned's next album ... I have a solid gold bed which I take on tour with me ... It's very unsatisfying and empty making love to five different girls in the same day!' Sometimes it happened, more often it did not and sometimes, sadly, you believed it had.

You were a master of self delusion and self publicity.

The media lapped you up and published all your dreams — facts or fiction. You were good copy and knew how to schmooze and booze. On one occasion when I set up an interview with you for Judith Simons of the *Daily Express*, she casually mentioned afterwards that she liked your hat. You bowed, took it off and gave it to her — Sir Walter Bolan. Good public relations.

Contrary to many people's belief, you were not a great drug taker. Your fantasies mostly came from sci-fi novels or dreams, and you took LSD only once to my knowledge by accident, when a drink was spiked. You hated smoking and when the joint was passed simply held your breath — you could not stand tobacco. But you loved pink champagne.

Perhaps one of oddest and most endearing memories associated with you and June was your adoration for the London Zoo gorilla called Guy who was a massive attraction during the sixties and seventies. Because your early flat in Maida Vale was close to the Zoo, you often walked there and Guy came to recognise both you and June from your regular visits. 'Sometimes we took him a cauliflower or some other treat,' you told me. 'He would go potty when he saw June. Anyway we got on close personal terms and then I became famous and a coach party of fans spotted us. June and I had to run. That was the end of our friendship with Guy — I really liked him. He reminded me of one of the directors at our record company.'

It was not until 'Hot Love', 'Get it On' and 'Telegram Sam' came out and Took was replaced by Mickey Finn that you switched from overgrown to underground and became what you was always wanted to be — a superstar. Some critics thought it was betrayal; I thought it was just a reversion to type, as you wanted to be a star at any cost. You were unrepentant when I interviewed you in 1970 for *NME* about your apparent conversion to mainstream pop. 'I got frightened by Jimi Hendrix at an early age,' you recalled. 'I managed to get on *Ready Steady Go* with my third record, "Hippy Gumbo", and it was Jimi's first appearance too. I took one look at what he was doing and it affected me so badly I went into rapid decline. Then I found myself as a member of a group called John's Children managed by Simon Napier Bell [Mr Bell was the man who later managed Japan and Wham] who suggested we got whips out on stage and pretended to beat each other — occasionally it got out of hand. I wrote as song for them called "Testimony" which got banned by the BBC and I am sure it would be now. It was a filthy record,' you added with great satisfaction.

'Sometimes I feel all the criticism of "teenage trivia" and rip-offs I am subjected to is just something I have to go through in some fatalistic way. I honestly feel it could all end tomorrow. Not just the band thing. I mean life. I could have my hands blown off and that would be it — whatever.'

There was an outrageously irreverent side to you that I loved. You once materialised backstage at the Rolling Stones concert at Wembley when I was also their press agent. You were ever so slightly tired and emotional and insisted on being ushered into Jagger's presence even though I requested you did not to push your luck in your present condition. Somehow you blagged your way into his dressing room. Suddenly, there was a scream of outrage from behind closed doors where 'His Jaggerness' had apparently been molested. 'Get him out of here,' bawled Mick. 'He just grabbed my balls.' You were gently but firmly lifted into the air by two enormous security men and rushed from the Presence. 'I didn't realise they were sacrosanct' you kept yelling out down the corridor. 'Put me down!' Thereafter, whilst I was representing both the Stones and yourself, you made a point of always enquiring how 'old golden bollocks' was.

There were curious moments in our own professional relationship, not the least of which was the day that you asked me to become your PR in 1972 as I was typing a feature for an American publication for which I was freelancing. I was working past 11 p.m. at night in my London office, something I rarely did, and the telephone rang. It was you in New York and you had heard I was doing some PR and wanted to know if I would like to help you.

'It is a weird coincidence that you should ring me right at this moment,' I said. 'Guess what I have just done?'

'I know,' you said. 'You have just written my name.' I had. Spooky.

My last abiding memories of you came from your early afternoon Granada TV show for which I travelled up with you each Thursday to Manchester. You told me after the last show that you intended to dump all the 'theatrical bullshit' and get back to working with some 'young punks who like to live dangerously and get on the road.' On your last show we travelled back with David Bowie on the train, who was extolling the talents of the writer Kurt Vonnegutt Jr and *Cats Cradle* which he was reading. 'Great title for a song,' you said to me. 'I am going to nick it.' You sadly never had time.

When I had suffered a minor heart attack in the seventies you were the one out of all my artistes who rang up and asked if you could just come in and help out in the office. Your heart was always in the right place even when you mislaid your head.

Wish you were here

Keith

PETE
TOWNSHEND

PETE TOWNSHEND

WHO WAS BEST

Dear Pete,

What can I say about our 18-year friendship? The bad temper, the crazed Mother, the drink and drug problems, the divorce, the verbal bullying, the strange love affair with Meher Baba, the violent altercations, the groupies, the thoughtless behaviour and the love–hate relationship with Entwistle, Moon and Daltrey — and that was just me!

In the beginning you were the original angry young man of the sixties, alienated by an establishment which had smugly informed us that 'you have never had it so good', and left a generation thrashing about like a beast with no head looking for a direction and something to bite. You empathised with the exasperation of the kids on the streets in dead-end jobs who were frustrated and needed to express their frustration, so waving the mods' flag of convenience you gave them a musical mirror and something to rally around.

The four Merseyside mop tops appeared to have rolled over and were having their tummies tickled by the likes of the Grade Organisation, and the Rolling

Stones appeared on *Sunday Night at The London Palladium*, albeit refusing to jump on the roundabout but still pandering to the screamage girls. The Who gave the boys something to yell about, and your first few singles 'I Can't Explain', 'Anyway Anyhow Anywhere' and 'My Generation' raised a collective howl of recognition from youth being processed through the dark maw of finding the dreaded 'Job'.

Your protestations and Daltrey's brilliant stuttering vocal (mods' speech patterns were often stammered due to the effects of purple hearts and speed) on 'My Generation' turned it into a rock and roll anthem, and The Who's aggressive style and gestalt feel gave the impression of a gang with whom you could identify rather than just another group.

It took only a few visits for the 'Tickets' and the 'Faces' who made up the mods' audience to recognise the anger being fed through the speakers and the physical force on-stage, for them to identify The Who as carrying the colours of their alienation. You identified with their confused angst and dissatisfaction, thrusting your guitar in their faces like a man with a flame-thrower in search of a match. You were an open invitation to a war party with the establishment, and your eloquence made you a natural spokesman for a generation who felt unrepresented and disenchanted with the status quo. You understood the power of anger and the impact that shattering a guitar could make on those who had little other means of expressing their dissatisfaction than physical aggression. The Who became a mouthpiece for a generation of strangulated, inarticulate, inhibited and spiritually bankrupt youth in the UK during the sixties, who were desperate to be seen and heard.

My first contact with you and The Who came via

your late co-manager Kit Lambert (the son of composer-arranger Constant Lambert), a gay, compassionate, lovable and at times completely insufferable alcoholic who, in fruity Noel Coward-like tones, talked me into coming along to the Marquee club in the early sixties 'to experience the next fucking sensation to follow the Beatles, dear boy.' His co-manager was Chris Stamp (brother of the actor Terence Stamp) who, as a streetwise Eastender, provided spine and business acumen.

I arrived at the Marquee on a wet Thursday night in 1964 to see posters advertising 'The Who — maximum R&B'. My name was not on the door as promised, and I had to pay the magnificent sum of seven and six pence to push my way through a bunch of sweaty mods in parkas and Fred Perry shirts with Hamlet-like hair cuts, but as I possessed my own 125cc Lambretta I felt curiously at home.

You had apparently suggested calling the band 'The Hair' at one stage, and Roger had wickedly suggested 'No One' because he liked the idea of someone having to say things like they would 'now like a big hand for No One.' There had a been a brief existence as The High Numbers and then The Detours and finally The Who.

On-stage there was a noise which sounded as though someone had been let loose with a chain-saw and was attempting to cut the microphone stand in half with his guitar, whilst a blonde thug up front sang 'I'm a man' over and over again and the out-of-time, pretty-boy drummer, who clearly belonged on another planet with another group, was doing his world famous impression of a souped-up octopus whilst an invisible bass player dressed in black desperately tried to keep time. In those days you could get John Entwistle in any colour as long as it was black (his tribute to Elvis) which extended to the hair. With white hair today, he looks like General Custer. Suddenly you went into your impression of Concorde or 'The Birdman' as it was contemporaneously known, arms spread wide and guitar apparently playing itself at an excruciating volume. I made for the exit. You were obviously all certifiable.

Just as I made the door, a hand with a cigarette in a holder plucked at my shoulder in the darkness and spun me around. 'Keithdearboyarenttheyfuckingincredible?' gabbled Kit. 'Come and have a brandy, then you must catch the finale — you will not believe it. This is a night you will remember for the rest of your life.' It was the brandy that persuaded me.

The finale was, of course, your impression of a four-man demolition squad which featured you splintering your guitar to smithereens on the stage, Entwistle ramming his bass through a speaker, Moon hurling drum sticks at Daltrey who responded by trying to knock him out with his own cymbal. As the dust settled and you stormed off in a flurry of feedback and murderous intent, sweat and splintered equipment, Kit took me aside and bellowed, 'Fucking amazing eh? I expect you would like to interview one of the boys now?'

What I wanted was a police escort off the premises to prevent any of you lunatics getting near me. However, I was persuaded to have a few words with Moon later in the bar who seemed the least psychotic (some mistake that was) but imparted that he must be off as the singer was threatening to kill him.

'Why?' I enquired.

'Coz I just told him he can't sing for shit,' smiled Moon engagingly, and exited stage left with a blonde. You did appear briefly but looked as though you were not keen on speaking to anyone, least of all a journalist.

There was, however, something compelling about the group and as the teen magazines I worked for were into 'pretty faces' I went back to Kit to fix an interview with Moon, for which of course he failed to turn up — so we reset at the *Ready Steady Go* TV show a few weeks later when he stalked into the canteen and produced a fireman's axe from his Adidas kit bag.

'What is that for?' I asked in alarm.

'That,' he said, 'is for Roger — haven't seen him have you?' It was always thus.

Sometimes your fights were for real, but more often they were merely letting off steam and letting the adrenalin settle. In the sixties the rows were often about money, or the lack of it, but they were also about performance because you all cared passionately about your stage work, and one thing I learnt quite early was never to go back to the Who's dressing room for half an hour after the concert. In there it was war — after every show there was a complete musical autopsy. Daltrey would have Moon by the throat. John would be trying to get in the middle and you would be threatening to break up the band unless things improved.

Much of the time Moon was your jester and you loved him as much for his incomparable drumming and psychopathic commitment to the band as the manic relief he provided from the stress and strains of touring, when you were all perpetually in debt and living hand-to-mouth. Quite apart from his outrageous behaviour, Moon was a clever improviser and mimic whom I remember once ad-libbed a routine based on 'The Owl and the Pussycat' in a huge empty cardboard box with you. It was prior to the Bangladesh charity concert at the Oval cricket ground, and kept everyone in hysterics for half an hour.

Yearly meetings with your accountant (an interesting man, permanently on the edge of a nervous breakdown, who appeared to drive cars up trees for a hobby) in Old Compton Street caused hysterics over the massive debts you were all under in the sixties as you waited for the royalties to catch up and Moon's expenses to go down. Keith was a one-man cruise missile who ran up massive expenses and did untold damage in hotels you could not afford. It is a testimony to how much he was loved and valued that the group always met his bills for damage when he was out of funds — which was most of the time.

On one occasion I was accompanying an American journalist going to interview Keith in a Los Angeles hotel, ushered along by tour manager Pete Rudge who came to a shuddering halt in the corridor outside one room, the blood drained from his face. The door to the room was hanging off the hinges and swinging crazily, while inside you could see the carpets were ripped up, large holes rent in the ceiling, windows out, light fittings wrenched from the wall and bits of furniture in a pile up against the window. Rudge scrabbled for his room list and then breathed a sigh of relief. 'Christ, I though it was Moon's room,' he said.

'Why?' asked the journalist.

'Because it looked like his room in San Francisco,' explained Rudge marching stoically onwards. On that occasion it was merely a hotel refurbishment in process, not Moon in action.

There was one farcical moment in the late sixties when you had finally got into the black financially, but by some strange book-keeping error Moon had been given half your royalties and, of course, joyfully spent them. You were less than enchanted with him at the yearly accountant's meeting when the facts emerged, and told him so. This caused him to storm out in high indignation, declaring he was quitting if anyone suspected him of stealing. He went officially missing for almost a week.

Eventually you received a reversed-charge phone call from the States in the early hours of the morning. You took the call on your bedside phone from a hideously drunk and genuinely distressed drummer. 'Pete, I'm sorry, Pete,' Keith slurred down the phone. 'You know I wouldn't spend your money deliberately, Pete. You know I love you, Pete. I'll pay it all back. I swear I will ... I didn't wake you did I?'

'No, Keith, I am always awake at 4.30 a.m. in the morning,' you responded, before telling him how everyone had been concerned and worried by his disappearance, that he sounded dreadful, and that he should forget about the money and just get something to eat. Suddenly down the phone came the noise of snoring. Moon had dropped off. You threw the receiver back on the phone in the darkness and went to sleep.

The following morning you had been shopping with your wife Karen in Twickenham and she tried to make a call from the phone in the kitchen but could get no dialling tone. You raced upstairs where the receiver was slightly off the hook, and picked it up to hear 'Zzzzzzzzzzzzzz' as Moon was still blissfully asleep at the other end, eight hours later, on his reversed-charge call to you from America.

You could hardly be said to have had it all your own way in The Who, despite your tendency to dominate, and Roger was not simply going to lie down and let intellect walk all over his common sense. Roger and you seldom seemed to appreciate why you were so good for each other, because of the aggravation and the pain of coming from opposite corners. In fact the group was a perfect mixture of opposite and contradictory characters which made life contentious but produced magic on stage, and to this day I have never heard a more perfect combination of guitar, bass, drums and vocals. On their best nights The Who simply flew. You had to have been there truly to understand.

I recall being sacked and reinstated as your press agent four times over eighteen years. Your tour manager John Woolf was quite put out at the time as he could only claim to have been sacked three times. My most notable rescue came from Moon who pleaded with you at a group AGM in Shepperton Studios not to dismiss me. 'Oh no, not KA — not after all these years,' adding wistfully, 'Couldn't we have him stuffed and put in a glass case in the corner of the board room.' I survived usually by simply ignoring the dismissal and carrying on — you almost inevitably forgave or forgot once the red mist had lifted, because you knew I loved the band.

One of my early tasks as PR in the seventies was to take the new MD from your American record company down to Shepperton where you were all rehearsing so he could meet you personally. We entered the sound stage while you were playing, just in time to witness Roger turn into the Incredible Hulk, throwing an immaculate right hook which sent you crashing to the stage with a sickening thud, knocking you unconscious. Roger was full of instant remorse, on his knees cradling your head and screaming for an ambulance whilst insisting he did not mean it and loved you. You seemed unaware of this.

'Holy shit,' exclaimed the horrified American MD, having witnessed the punch-up whilst waiting for me to introduce him to you. 'Are they always like this?'

'No,' I responded nonchalantly. 'Today is one of

their better days — shall we repair to the bar until all the judges votes have been counted?'

The Who were like one of those damaging, volatile marriages that we encounter which are based on permanent, feuding, vicious rows ('all sound and fury signifying something'), crockery hurled at each other's heads but underpinned by a passionate and almost unshakeable love that no one else fully understands, least of all the contestants. Your most stable member appeared to be John Entwistle, who was also the most gifted musician and he at least seem to have one foot on the ground, even if his eccentricities stretched to living in a semi-detached house in Ealing which bore a passing resemblance to an anti-room in Hampton Court Palace with suits of armour, tapestries, model Spanish galleons with silver sails (which kept being burglarised). There was also an ornamental fountain together with life-size statues of his Irish wolf hounds in the garden, and pet tarantulas. The man next door kept chickens. Now John is deaf and slightly potty, rattling around in a huge manor house in the Cotswolds whose hall is graced by a life-size model of Quasimodo hanging from a bell rope. God preserve the loveable eccentrics of this world like the Ox.

The most immediate impressions most people had of you over the years was of an intellect (rare in rock and roll) sliced with anger and compassion. Your rage is often taken out on friends, whilst your enemies, for whom you have little time, seem to escape the whipping. Bobby Pridden, who became an inspired sound man with The Who and others, was often the subject of some dreadful tirades from you on-stage and off. Yet I doubt if there are many people you cared more about then or now. I was similarly screamed at, sacked and reduced to tears, but it seemed like a bollocking from you was almost confirmation of our existence; we minions bore them like a long-term service medal. Despite all the tantrums and bad behaviour The Who had one of the longest-serving and devoted management and promotional teams in the business. Still do, when needed.

My very first trip to America in 1966 was courtesy of you and Jimi Hendrix who paid for my air tickets. I flew out with Jimi, and we spent time in New York before eventually meeting up with you at the Monterey Festival. The Who were amazing, and you appeared through a fog of dry ice on-stage dressed in a blue sequined Edwardian jacket with white ruffles and a pearl-encrusted jacket looking like a cross between Lord Byron and the Marquis de Sade. Sometimes you behaved like them. The Who poleaxed the festival audience who were shell-shocked by the destruction that marked the finale, with Moon putting his personal stamp on proceedings by kicking his bass drum into the press pit. As the splinters from your guitar were still drifting downwards the American roadies ran bewildered amongst the wreckage trying to save their house PA system.

I was delighted with your triumph which I was reporting for *NME*, and told you so later when we met up for a connecting flight to LA. But you gave me a bollocking for spending too much time with Jimi and not enough with The Who. 'Who's paying for your return flight anyway,' you snarled. I was mortified and explained I would be treating you equally. What I really felt like doing was punching you on your famous nose.

Pettyness is not normally one of your flaws, and I have seldom walked away from a conversation with you without something worthwhile to contemplate. You have always given of your time even when under pressure, and despite the odd tantrum I have yet to encounter any other artiste of your stature, intellect or compassion. On a personal level, when I broke my leg playing football and was hospitalised for six weeks you were the only artiste to turn up and visit from my roster of superstars, with a thoughtful collection of tapes, fruit and flowers.

Unlike other supergroups it would take a calculator to tot up the number of charity concerts and millions you have raised for charity with The Who. I note from a local paper you are still giving time regularly to a young offenders prison to advise and encourage them with their in- house radio and DJ work. The Who were one major group who never went into tax exile, although of course Moon, who loved a fashionable trait, claimed to have done so at one time, despite being bankrupt.

Years ago, when you were going through the hell of drug addiction and we were all at our wits end trying to stop you turning into the person you had always warned us not to become, I swore then that if this killer of business destroyed you, then I would quit and become a postman or a milkman or anything. Fortunately you had suffecent mental strength to drag yourself back — and you also unfortunately had friends and family who were not content to watch you destroy yourself.

Having written and produced the world's first rock opera with *Tommy*, a double album which actually made number one in the American charts on three separate occasions, firstly with The Who and then Lou Reisner's 'all-star' orchestrated version and finally as the soundtrack to Ken Russell's *Tommy* movie, it was not surprising to see you reinvent it as a successful Broadway musical and then bring it into the West End.

With wonderful solo albums like *Empty Glass* behind you, collaborations with the late Ted Hughes on *The Iron Man* at the Young Vic and the occasional appearances with your own band as Pete Townshend and Friends, you are still very much with us. Now it seems you have picked up the pieces of the 'Lifehouse' project for which I worked with you as your PR in the seventies, and the diamond-like splinters of what went into one of the Who's finest albums *Who's Next* and provided the songs, 'Won't Get Fooled Again', 'Behind Blue Eyes' and 'Baba O'Riley.'

At that time you were anticipating the Internet called it 'The Grid', as well as the IT technology which is now almost taken for granted, in addition to virtual reality. It was a disturbingly brilliant piece of prophecy and too advanced for most of us to grasp from the Young Vic Concerts where you put your abstractions to the test and they failed to gel. You tend always to be ahead of the game and your great need has been someone to put your visionary ideas into practical reality.

You are, quite simply, the most conscientious and impressive artiste I have worked for in the music business, and you led the best live band ever — but you ain't perfect, so there. Keep on keeping on.

Love

Keith

POSTCARDS
FROM THE EDGE

Dear Other Clients,

For those of you disappointed at not being pilloried here due to lack of space, may I just add a few postscripts about my impressions of others who graced the books of KA Publicity?

MANFRED MANN

South African born, you were either a Boer or a boor, or a bore I was never sure. I had the dubious pleasure of looking after your jazz-blues band Chapter III in the seventies, with your long-suffering drummer Mike Hugg. Arrogance personified you once required me to give you a road by road run down on how to find the *Daily Mirror* building by push bike, and then had the gall to inform the interviewer in front of me that you assumed that I had nothing to do with setting up the interview. The journalist was non-plussed, but admitted I had talked him into it. Thank you, Don Short.

THE STRANGLERS

You never successfully replaced your gifted songwriter and vocalist Hugh Cornwell when I re-inherited you in the nineties. We briefly represented you in the seventies when my assistant Alan Edwards did the hard work on your first *Rattus Norvegicus* album. Your new singer, Paul Roberts, had a good voice but did not possess the menace and songwriting prowess of his predecessor.

Paul looked like Oliver Twist sent to play on death row with the Krays. Jean Jacques was an unpredictable karate-kicking bassist. Drummer Jet Black lived in a converted railway station and keyboard player Dave Greenfield memorably cancelled a gig when his pet rat died. SOS Hugh.

THE DAMNED

You could have taken over where Screaming Lord Sutch left off, but no talented drummer deserves to live through middle age with the name of Rat Scabies. I saw you recently on a Channel 4 talk show scarlet with embarrassment when they tried to make you jump about on a stupid pogo stick and you hid behind the pillar. I saw you, Chris Miller! Singer Dave Vanian seemed desperate to be a vampire — maybe he was. Guitarist Brian James was just desperate.

BILL WYMAN

Eternally chewing gum, immobile and holding his bass as though he were shooting grouse. Bill was a permanent fixture in the Stones who they now miss more than they care to admit. I looked after your Sticky Fingers restaurant for a year and helped out with the Mandy Smith saga, or was it sago? Marrying a young girl is not a capital offence and love can make fools of us all. Bill is not known to forget a slight or an insult easily, but I like him and he once lent me a pair of his socks when I ran out on a tour I covered for the Stones in the sixties. Sock and Roll!

IAN GILLAN

You were Deep Purple's finest lead vocalist who sang on the classic 'Smoke on the Water'. One of the boys. Not Ritchie Blackmore's greatest fan. Gentle, with a streak of alarming vulgarity. Have a curious but endearing hobby of re-marrying your wife Bron in every new country you visit under their respective marital law, and you like to dress in the traditional style of the country. Why not?

THE PRETTY THINGS

You are outrageous old rockers who in the sixties incorporated an early Stones bass player in Dick Taylor, when your vocalist Phil May was even prettier than Jagger. He distinguished himself by being deported from New Zealand. You had a smart manager in Mark St John who also produced and doubled on drums. Too late now, I fear.

HAWKWIND

You seemed permanently out to lunch, or in outer space. On the strength of one big hit single 'Silver Machine' you became a sort of acid house *Star Trek*. Represented you for a few months in the seventies, but impossible to co-ordinate. I liked your eccentric sax player Nik Turner, when he remembered to turn up, and your vocalist the late Robert Calvert was hugely amusing and wrote an underrated 'faction' on the business called *Hype*. Mad hippies.

PETER TOSH

You were the supremely talented Wailer with Bob Marley and then a star with your own band whom I had for the *Mystic Man* album. Mad as a March hare. I met you at Heathrow Airport and you informed me you had a magic stick, given to you by a man in a UFO, which when you pointed it at people made them vanish. It worked a treat with me. Pity it did not work with the man who pointed the gun at you.

ALVIN LEE

You were so laid back you seemed asleep, and were once the fastest guitarist in the West. You made your name with 'Ten Years After' in the Woodstock movie. When I inherited you in the seventies you had become Alvin Lee and Co, and seemed to be under the delusion that if you put on your carpet slippers, walked from your kitchen, to your recording studio in the barn outside your Henley mansion, you could make inspired blues music. Wrong.

HERMAN

You were the pompous little pop idol I inherited in the seventies who had 'No Milk Today'. After you shook off the the Hermits and Mickie Most you were determined to do just as well as Peter Noone. Did not.

MIDGE URE

I represented you during your time with your teenage idols group Slik from whom you escaped to form Ultravox. Tried to hang on to you because I knew you had talent, but you never seemed to care desperately about success to stay with it too long. You deserved enormous credit for backing Bob Geldof during Band Aid which was one of the few occasions I felt proud of the pop music business. One of the good guys.

STRAY CATS

My only other excursion into management, other than Andy Fairweather-Low, was your little trio from New York in 1986 whom I discovered sleeping on the floor of my office in Old Compton Street. My PA Claudine had rightly devised that there was something special about you, and you had nowhere to go and were stoney broke.

    I organised some rehearsal time for you and once I

clapped eyes on Setzer in action I thought it was Eddie Cochran come back to haunt me. (Years later you played Cochran in the film *La Bamba*). Setzer was electrifying and the old slapback bass rock and roll you played was the rockabilly style of the fifties brought into the eighties. I was offered a contract to co-manage you and brokered a lucrative deal for you with CBS Records before departing on holiday.

When I returned it had become a rock and roll nightmare. My co-manager had moved in another record company and the dealers, groupies and crooked accountants were in the dressing room. All the parasites and sycophants I had spent time avoiding for the past twenty years had gathered in my absence. I walked out and Jim asked where I was going. 'To get Frederico Fellini to direct the movie,' I said, but it fell on deaf ears.

Now I see that Brian is going great guns in the States as he fronts his own swing band in the vanguard of the return of the big bands. Don't count on it lasting long, Brian — it is too expensive and unwieldy these days too carry that amount of people and baggage, but yo — a rock and roll Count Basie is no bad idea. Just try and justify the expense to the bean counters.

Some day we must meet up and you must explain to me how your drummer wound up with Brit Eckland. From Peter Sellers to Rod Stewart to Slim Jim Phantom. She has to go for a Womble next. Uncle Bulgaria is, to the best of my knowledge, still available.